THE GROUP DYNAMIC FIELD GUIDE FOR YOUTH

THE GROUP DYNAMIC FIELD GUIDE FOR YOUTH

51 Ideas Student Leaders Can Use Today!

ALAN D FEIRER

The Group Dynamic Field Guide for Youth

51 Ideas Young Leaders can Use Today

Group Dynamic Publications
1128 W Jefferson St
Winterset, IA 50273

Ordering Information:
Quantity sales. Special discounts are available on quantity purchases by corporations, associations, and others. For details, contact the publisher at the address above.

First Edition

ISBN-13: 9781539463429 (Group Dynamic Publications)
ISBN-10: 1539463427

Cover design by Jordan Kuhns Design.
Cover Photograph © 2015 iStock by Preto Perola.

DEDICATION...

My beloved wife, Julie Feirer, who supports, encourages, and challenges me, and changed the name of my business from "Beyond Introductions" to "Group Dynamic." Thousands thank her for that, I'm sure.

My hard-working daughter, Mara Feirer, who challenges, encourages, and supports me. She is on her way to being a great leader, and many days, she leads me.

My amazing mother, Sally Wilke, who always made me feel like I could do anything, and has inspired me with her life's work as a servant to others, generally those living in difficult circumstances.

Rebecca Pottebaum, who was one of the most powerful student leaders I've known. She showed me—and her peers—what a youth leader is capable of. By the way, Becky, they still do the attitude check. Fourteen years and three directors later.

Dr. Art Sunleaf, who was one of my first challengers, supporters, and encouragers, and helped create the familiar "Group Dynamic Triangle." The full story is at the end.

TABLE OF CONTENTS

FOREWORD

by Dr. Tim Lautzenheiser

"The future-of-tomorrow lies within our youth-of-today."

KUDOS to Alan Feirer for his unprecedented commitment and exemplary dedication focused on student leadership; his endless efforts are paying priceless dividends to those who are fortunate enough to be in one of his acclaimed workshops, or as a benefactor of the knowledge shared in his mission-driven books. We are all indebted to this innately gifted teacher, mentor, master.

The Group Dynamic Field Guide for Youth is yet another worthy contribution to support the ongoing journey of positive learning-growing-becoming. Not only does Mr. Feirer offer steadfast wisdom concerning the ever-growing field of leadership development, but he also has framed it in a sequential curriculum designed for the reader to "take action" on the various servitude mantras strategically integrated in each and every chapter.

What is excitingly unique about the book you are holding is the signature style-of-writing reflecting the affable, caring personality of the author. One can quickly embrace the content since it is delivered in a user-friendly fashion that can be immediately applied to the challenges we all face in our personal and professional development. As you go from page-to-page, you will find yourself nodding-in-agreement about a highlighted concept, pondering how this-or-that idea can be adapted to your own situation, and being solidly convinced you CAN "make a difference" by serving those around you.

Of particular interest is the: Rate yourself – and ask others to rate you – on this: segment at the end of each chapter. These reflective evaluations afford serious introspection, and also the chance for others to share their perspective. This self-imposed exercise guarantees LASTING POWER that can be tapped today, tomorrow, and forever.

I invite you to "take your time" as you consume the well-written ideas unselfishly brought to the table by Alan. Read a paragraph, then take a moment to think about the WHY, HOW and WHAT it can bring to all forums of life. Mr. Feirer has written as much between-the-lines as on-the-lines; take advantage of every delicious morsel-of-understanding he serves-up.

CONGRATULATIONS to Alan Feirer for this treasured gift, and CONGRATULATIONS to YOU for adding it to your personal leadership library of cornerstone texts. May we always be reminded: Leadership isn't something we do; leadership is something we are.

INTRODUCTION

"**W**ait a second- didn't you already write this book, for grown-ups? Aren't you just giving us the same book, redone for student leaders?"

Yup.

When I started working in the area of leadership development, it was with young people. And, the material I used with students did not come from "youth" leadership experts - it came from leadership experts, who geared their material toward the corporate world.

So, I took that material and translated it into the worlds that young people occupy. It didn't take much work, because student leaders are far more capable than they are given credit for.

But you know that. You're reading this book.

Leadership is the act of meeting needs. If this is true, then leaders need ideas to put into action now. The next step is clear: Provide this book for those leaders.

And whether we are just beginning or continuing to explore and develop leaders, we can all turn to this two-word action plan for effective leadership as a touchstone:

MEET NEEDS.

Meeting needs requires curiosity. A leader has to ask, "What's needed?" and then act on it.

Depending on the situation, variations on this question could be...

"What does she need from me?"

"What does this team need right now?"

"What does he/she need to hear to do his/her best work?"

And so on.

The answer a leader comes up with might be 100% right on, but more likely it's just close: 50-80% right on. Still, the resulting actions will be a better choice than acting on your gut instinct.

THE THREE STEP PROCESS.

To get into a position to meet the needs of others, student leaders must do these three things, in this order:

1) Build Relationships
2) Encourage Others
3) Ask for More

Each of the 50 readings in this book help you be more effective with one or more of those three steps.

A word about words:

This book is for all student leaders. Think student council, Key club, band, basketball, speech, FBLA, NHS… *all* of them.

Sometimes the words I use don't fit everything. If this were only about sports, I'd only use sports examples, and use the word "team" more. If this were only about band, I'd use a lot of marching band examples, and use the word "section" more. If this were only about service clubs, I'd use a lot of club and committee examples, and use the word "club" more.

Instead, I mix it up. And assume that because you have the self-discipline to read and apply this, you also have the smarts to see how *any* example in here can apply to your activities.

As you read this book, consider a bias toward **action**. The world moves when we do. Lack of initiative doesn't result in lack of change; it results in decay. It all comes down to "what's needed now."

HOW TO USE THIS BOOK

Here are some suggestions for reading and applying this material, based on your individual needs and available time.

1. Read it beginning to end, but pause to complete each reflection question, and ask a teacher, coach, director, and/or older student leader to share their thoughts on your self-perception.

2. Embrace just one segment per week, on Sunday, and complete the reflection question. Stay focused on that question during your week. On Wednesday afternoon or Thursday morning, ask a teacher, coach, director, and/or older student leader to rate you on that reflection question, then implement their feedback the rest of the week.

3. Rate yourself on all the reflection questions first, then start reading the segments in which you've rated yourself the lowest.

4. Skim the Table of Contents and mark the 5 segments that seem the most interesting. Read those in one week, one per day. Then, the next week, stay focused on those 5. Repeat the process 9 more times until you've digested the first 50.

Regardless of how you approach it, reflection and discussion with a trusted person or two are important for embracing the concepts presented. I recommend an adult, and an experienced fellow student.

THE EIGHT POINT LEADERSHIP MODEL

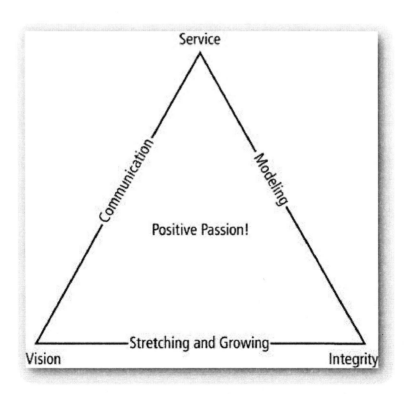

The points represent the three-legged stool of leadership mindsets: Leaders must have a commitment to <u>service</u>, clear <u>vision</u>, and consistent <u>integrity</u>.

The legs connect the mindsets with visible implementation: Leaders master <u>communication</u>, consistently <u>modeling</u> what is expected, and commit to <u>stretching and growing</u>.

In the middle, the constant display of <u>passion</u>, expressed in <u>positive</u> ways.

For the curious, the origin story of the model is in the Afterword. For now, let's take action and dig in to Service.

SECTION ONE: SERVICE

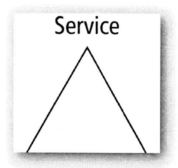

Service

The essence of leadership is service.

The idea that service is essential to the role of a leader is not new. Author Robert Greenleaf paved the way for opening minds to this concept a few decades ago, and now the concept is quite widely accepted.

When approaching any individual, any team, any organization – a good leader asks, "What is needed?" rather than, "What am I supposed to do now to maintain control?"

Have you ever had a bad teacher, coach, or boss? Probably. But here is something that happens regularly:

Someone is good at something, and they end up becoming a leader because of it, even though the skills needed for leadership are different than the skills they've mastered.

For example, Ben the grocery store employee might be very good at working in the produce and dairy sections, rotating items correctly, showing up for work on time, and following orders. Because of this, he gets promoted to produce supervisor. Now, he's supposed to get *others* to rotate items, show up on time, and follow orders. But that requires different skills. This happens all the time.

This often results in a misunderstanding of how to lead. It becomes very easy for someone to become a leader and think, "I'm in charge."

That idea is not completely wrong. It's okay to be "in charge". The problem is that it can lead to other assumptions like, "These people had better do what I say. They'd better respect my authority. There's a lot of pressure on me to make sure everyone gets the job done." These thoughts may be true, but they keep the focus on the leader, not the organization and its members, where it should be.

Acting from a place of serving and meeting needs just plain works, but we can't stop there. How do we really determine what is needed? Then, how exactly do we do that?

We can't stop with, "A leader serves", but it is where we start. Instead of thinking, "I've done my share," think, "What more can be done?"

"...be authentic, be vulnerable, be present, be accepting, and be useful. And by useful I mean, be servants." – James Autry

Rate yourself – and ask others to rate you – on this:

When approaching a situation, I actively seek to find out what is needed of me, rather than what I can do to maintain control.

(low)   1   2   3   4   5   (high)

Self-perception:

_____

_____

_____

Feedback from others:

_____

_____

_____

_____

_____

1

• • •

MEET NEEDS

I ate in a London pub with a group of music students once, and the server made a mistake when calculating the bill. Unfortunately, he didn't believe us, and the ensuing argument kept escalating.

Confession: I got a little... um... animated.

He was in the wrong (I have witnesses), but now he had a service issue with an obviously upset customer (me), so he pulled out the last resort at his disposal:

"What do you want me to do, exactly?"

Great question! Hearing this calmed me down and gave me the chance to stop listing facts, numbers, and the order of events, and simply say:

"Acknowledge that Daniel has paid, and stop trying to charge him twice."

The server then proceeded to do a lot of slamming around of change and drawers, and told us never to come back, but Daniel was spared being double-charged.

This story isn't about leadership directly, but it can be adapted to illustrate an important instruction:

At points of exasperation, when you're tempted to escalate or argue, why not stop and ask: "What do you need that you're not getting?"

Answers to this question could surprise you, help you, and allow you to serve your follower(s) with less tension and greater speed as long as you are sincere when asking.

Also – and this is big – it can reinforce the connection between you and your peer followers. Remember, you are seeking the chance to *meet needs*, which is your ultimate responsibility as a leader.

Real-world answers to this question that I have personally heard, or heard about:

"Respect from you."

"Water."

"...for people to stop taking my equipment without asking."

Once you have an answer, you can move forward. Sometimes you can satisfy a reasonable request; sometimes the answer is real, but unrelated to the original topic; sometimes the request is totally unreasonable.

Even if you can't immediately act on the answer, you've gotten to the bottom of things to a greater extent, shown concern for needs, and slowed things down. You're closer to solving the problem and getting back to work.

Rate yourself – and ask others to rate you – on this:

When I sense conflict or tension, I ask variations of "What do you need that you are not getting?"

(low)   1   2   3   4   5   (high)

Self-perception:

_____

_____

_____

Feedback from others:

_____

_____

_____

_____

_____

2

ADDRESS THIS COMMON OBSTACLE

Dr. Tim Lautzenheiser, the internationally renowned music educator and speaker, coined the concept of The Four Levels of Maturity.

The Four Levels of Maturity is an easy-to-grasp simplification of some basic psychological concepts.

Combining this way of looking at maturity with the concepts in a great business book *Leadership and Self-Deception* (from The Arbinger Institute) has proven to be a very effective way to help people learn how to tolerate other people.

It's also a great tool for personal growth and better leadership.

LEVEL I: SELFISH ("WHAT'S IN IT FOR ME?")

Behaviors on this level are focused entirely on gratification. Examples of this behavior include ignoring housekeeping tasks, being late, answering your cell phone or texting in the middle of a conversation, not flushing a public toilet because you don't feel like touching the handle, etc. These are all selfish behaviors, executed with little regard for the impact they may have on others.

LEVEL II: INDEPENDENT ("I'LL DO MY JOB – BUT THAT'S IT.")

This level is most dangerous, because when we behave at this level, we *think* we're a team player, because we're technically following the rules. The mindset here is, "I've taken care of all my stuff. It doesn't matter to me if you have done the same. None of my business." Behaviors at this level include cleaning up your own mess, but walking past other messes; being on time, but not offering a ride to someone else who might also be late, finishing your part of the group project ahead of schedule, but failing to offer help to those who are a bit behind – "Not my problem, not my fault."

The first two levels are both self-centered, with no real regard for the team, or for other people in the world.

You will hear me refer to these two levels as acting "below the line." You don't want to be there.

LEVEL III: COOPERATIVE (BEING EMPATHETIC AND EFFECTIVE)

Behaviors at this level include working together according to everyone's strengths, weaknesses and capabilities, to get things done for the team, or the world at large. "I'll pick up this stuff, if you hold the door for me" or "I'll make the locker signs for the team if you get Brittney to help put them up after school." Most successful groups see these behaviors relatively frequently from their members, and nearly all the time from their leaders. This is where we land when we're being easy to work with. But – the most effective leaders and team members cannot rest at this level, because there will always be people acting at levels one and two "below the line".

LEVEL IV: GIVING (ACTIVELY FINDING AND MEETING NEEDS)

Acting at this level means you have made a consistent commitment to meeting the needs of others, and of the group, in order to get things done. It isn't about being a pushover, or enabling selfish behaviors in others, but an acknowledgment that many people have habitual behaviors at levels one and two.

When people are "below the line," or acting at levels one and two, there is absolutely no patient way to get them to grow up and act at levels three and four.

While there is no *efficient* way to do this, there is an *effective* way – by constantly acting "above the line". That is, constantly demonstrate behaviors at levels three and four.

Rate yourself – and ask others to rate you – on this:

I actively work to operate within maturity Levels III and IV, and encourage others to do so as well.

(low)   1   2   3   4   5   (high)

Self-perception:

_____

_____

_____

Feedback from others:

_____

_____

_____

_____

_____

3

LISTEN MORE. TALK LESS. PAUSE AND LEARN.

Leaders often know what the needs are in a situation, and dictate them with authority. While the leader is often correct about the direction, engagement can suffer without more buy-in. Asking questions that help others discover the same needs can help.

Even when you know what is needed, consider expanding your own understanding, helping others buy in and be a part of the process by asking questions similar to these:

What do you think we should do next?

Is this situation similar to anything we've ever seen before?

If you were in my shoes, what would you suggest we do now?

If I moved to a new school, and you got put in charge of this, what would you do?

For example, it's become clear that Friday afternoon sectionals are less effective than the Wednesday early morning meetings. If you have a team member that you need to build a relationship with, or who feels like s/he isn't always heard,"consider asking that person "If you were in charge of scheduling these sectionals, would you leave them on Friday, or just have them all on Wednesday?"

The answer will probably be the solution you've considered, so now you've build trust with them by adopting their idea. And if the answer is different, you'll learn something. For example, they may come back with "Wednesday seems like the better idea, because those always go better, but sometimes we get new music on Thursday in class, so a Friday sectional makes more sense most of the time. What if we tried them Thursday night, though?"

In *Winning*, former General Electric Chief Executive Officer Jack Welch points out that listening more and talking less helps to meet needs:

> *"Obviously, some people have better ideas than others; some people are smarter or more experienced or more creative. But, everyone should be heard and respected. They want it, and you need it."*

Leaders need to listen more, talk less, and learn.

Rate yourself – and ask others to rate you – on this:

I make time to question others about their viewpoints, and listen to their ideas, concerns, and opinions.

(low)   1   2   3   4   5   (high)

Self-perception:

_____

_____

_____

Feedback from others:

_____

_____

_____

_____

_____

4

• • •

KNOW ROLE POWER V. RELATIONSHIP POWER

saw a Disney cast member holler at a child once - and it was perfectly appropriate. Have you been to a Disney Park? If so, you know...

Disney cast members are highly trained in many ways. You likely know of their magical customer service and commitment to staying in character. They also make sure the parks run smoothly, but the order in which all of these commitments play out is not at all random.

Disney gives all staff (they call them "cast" because they're always putting on a "show") a clear priority order of their Basics, or Keys:

1. Safety
2. Courtesy
3. Show
4. Efficiency

If everything is going well – no safety issues, everyone is cooperating, and there are no challenges to staying "in character," then cast members are free to do whatever is most efficient to get things moving quickly for guests, whether it's a line, or food, or a character interaction.

However, they will let efficiency slide to keep the "show" intact – to stay in character. If you eat at the 50s Prime Time Cafe, part of the show is that they bring you nothing unless you say "please". For everything. I asked for "Diet Coke, and water, please" and she brought me only the water. "Still waiting for that Diet Coke," I said a few times, until I realized that I had never paired "Diet Coke" with "please". Once I did, there it was. Our server came around and hovered a lot to give me the opportunity - totally inefficient, but part of the show, and my daughter loved it.

The show may slide for the sake of courtesy. The cast at The Haunted Mansion is glum and stern, and a bit creepy. The ride itself isn't that scary, and when a small child started crying in line, a cast member broke character, took the child aside, sat on the curb with her, and explained – you may even say spoiled – every single effect and visual of the attraction. The cast member smiled, encouraged, and patiently explained. Courtesy trumps show.

On the Winnie the Pooh attraction, a toddler ahead of me worked his way out from under the lap bar in his Hunny Pot and started to stand on the seat, so quickly that there was no time to politely modify his behavior.

"HEY! SIT DOWN! SIT DOWN *NOW*!" hollered the cast member - out of character, not in show, not efficient (she stopped letting people on the attraction in those moments), and certainly not courteous.

The toddler obeyed, and we were all shaken up, but it made perfect sense. Safety is huge at Disney - and should be for you, too. A safe culture frees people from fear.

What's the lesson here for a student leader?

A clear priority of what you need to be most mindful of in any given situation. Maybe you don't have to watch for Safety, Courtesy, Show, and Efficiency.

Even though you're not running Disney World, you can learn from the best and apply those lessons in *your* world.

For example, if you're a leader in choir, maybe the priorities are:

1. Make sure everyone stays informed and feels included.
2. Make sure everyone knows their music.

If you know those are the priorities, then you'll offer to help people with their music. Or, you'll watch to see if someone doesn't understand when the arrival time for the concerts are, then offer rides or give information to those who seem like they don't "get it."

Rate yourself – and ask others to rate you – on this:

I remain alert and attentive to what my first priority is day-to-day. Should I be attending to one priority (efficiency) and a major concern arises (safety), I quickly shift direction to take care of that need.

(low)　　1　　2　　3　　4　　5　　(high)

Self-perception:

_____

_____

_____

Feedback from others:

_____

_____

_____

_____

_____

5

ASK THIS IMPORTANT QUESTION

If the two-word action plan for leadership is "meet needs," then you have frequent opportunities to be very explicit about that mission by taking just three seconds to ask some variation of:

"Is there anything I can do to help you with that?"

Variations to get you started:

"Can I show you how?"

"Would you like help?"

"What if I send you a reminder?"

If any command, criticism, new instruction, behavior-outcome statement (we'll cover this in reading 16), or problem identification is immediately followed by this willingness to help, you will provide safety and assistance for those you serve.

Some people say that helping people will only make them less capable of showing initiative on their own, but I disagree. Working with people to solve problems, and teaching them to do so, will lead to greater independence and better relationships in the future. They will only show more individual initiative when you show them how to do so.

If you're correcting punctuality issues, offer a reminder alert. If you're addressing sloppy effort, work very hard yourself to show them what to do. If disrespect is the issue, offer to give them a signal to remind them they're falling back into old habits.

Try this for a couple weeks, and see what happens. "Is there anything I can do to help you with that?" Use it cautiously, however; if the task is very simple, or if you have the wrong tone, this could come across sarcastically.

Rate yourself – and ask others to rate you – on this:

I intentionally and frequently ask my team variations of, "What can I do to help you with that?" especially after making a request or providing critical feedback.

(low)　　1　　2　　3　　4　　5　　(high)

Self-perception:

_____

_____

_____

Feedback from others:

_____

_____

_____

_____

SECTION TWO: VISION

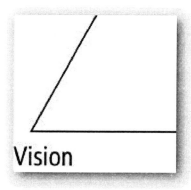

Vision

Effective leaders must have vision. Not just in the "creatively imagined future" way, but also in the way of "I hold an accurate view of the way things are right now."

Leaders must inspire a shared vision. Without knowing what the goals are, people are rarely motivated.

While much is often made of that "creatively imagined future" form of vision, some leaders neglect the need to accurately figure out the "here and now".

Motivation toward goals will erode when the leader is out of touch with the current state of affairs; an overly optimistic leader can turn people off if they ignore problems. On the other hand, an overly pessimistic leader can bring down morale.

In setting goals, and developing the "future" sense of vision, many organizational leaders are already familiar with SWOT activities — these are good, and make sense.

In this section, we'll look more closely at this. The "Three Things" activity I'll share next is one way to get others to join you to develop goals and explore vision, and it can build a bridge between the present and the future.

Where are you going? Whether it's simple or complex, make sure there's an answer to that question.

> **"The best coaches know what the end result looks like ... if you don't know what the end result looks like, you can't get there." – Vince Lombardi**

Rate yourself – and ask others to rate you – on this:

I can accurately describe both

    A) *the ideal state of our group and*
    B) *the exact current state of our group.*

(low)   1   2   3   4   5   (high)

Self-perception:

_____

_____

_____

Feedback from others:

_____

_____

_____

_____

_____

6

LEARN TO BE VISIONARY

Let's start with the Three Things activity. This is something I learned and adapted from Dr. Tim Lautzenheiser, the legendary youth leadership speaker.

STEP ONE – Make two lists, of three items each:

1) List three words or phrases that describe your organization as it *is now*, <u>but you wish were not true</u>.

2) List three words or phrases you *wish* would describe your organization, but that <u>aren't true now</u>.

For example, here were my responses in a high school band program I was once associated with:

1. pessimistic, stressed people, culture of fear [current reality – not desirable]
2. forward-thinking, celebratory, high-achieving
[ideal reality – what's desired]

STEP TWO – Look in the mirror, and ask, "Which of these six words or phrases describe ME?"

Then write them down.

For example: Honestly, I was pessimistic, and one of the stressed people, but I was also forward-thinking.

STEP THREE – Set a goal for yourself to either...

1) Eliminate one of the undesirables, or 2) take on one of the desirables.

For example: I could have made a goal for myself to stop my pessimistic behaviors — to never again say anything about possible drama, or the gloom of the current situation.

By doing so, you become part of the solution, not part of the problem.

Also, you've taken a step in developing your own concept of **vision** — the ability to honestly assess the current state, and imaginatively picture the ideal state.

What if everyone in your organization/team did this exercise?

Rate yourself – and ask others to rate you – on this:

Based on where my team is right now, and where I know they need to be, I take active measures to get us from point A to point B.

(low)   1   2   3   4   5   (high)

Self-perception:

_____

_____

_____

Feedback from others:

_____

_____

_____

_____

_____

7

KNOW THE VALUE IN RUBRICS

We all need a starting point for discussions about vision, direction, and goals. That's precisely why many of your best teachers love to use rubrics as scoring tools: Simple rubrics are easy to create and use, and help make things clear.

Consider using a scale of 1 to 3, or 1 to 5, to keep them simple.

Rubric Example 1

You're considering peers for a leadership position in your Key Club, and they're all good.

Start by listing your values, or other traits you're looking for, in one column on a spreadsheet.

Put the names of the candidates at the top. Then, rate them all on a scale of 1 to 5 for each value or desired trait.

You'll quickly see who scores the highest, or the lowest, and can use that as a starting point.

Rubric Example 2

Your student council is overwhelmed.

You've come up with all sorts of great ideas for your school, and because everyone is busy, there's too much to accomplish realistically.

Rate all the project ideas on a scale of 1 to 3.

List the projects on the top row. And in the left column, list these criteria:

- Value to School (makes this a great place to come each day for both students and teachers)
- Value to Students (makes student spirit better)
- Value to Community (gets notice from the local newspaper, parents, or other concerned citizens)

Looking at your projects this way will help you prioritize where to put your efforts first.

And, if something reveals itself as not urgent, it's a good time to end the effort— or put it on a list for next year.

Rubric Example 3

Feeling a lack of direction? Every day, I apply a rubric to my to-do list.

I mark items with an "A" if they must be done today, "B" if they ought to be done this week, and "C" if they require attention, but aren't that urgent.

Overwhelmed? Create a rubric.

Rate yourself – and ask others to rate you – on this:

I make use of simple rubrics to help myself, and my team, get clarity of direction when needed.

(low)   1   2   3   4   5   (high)

Self-perception:

_____

_____

_____

Feedback from others:

_____

_____

_____

_____

_____

8

REPORT BY COLOR TO KEEP IT SIMPLE

Have you ever been part of a club or team that had so many ideas and projects that it was hard to keep them straight?

Many times, these plans and initiatives go above and beyond the day-to-day work of busy student leaders.

Because of that, sometimes those plans never get put into action, or the work on them falls behind, or gets sloppy.

As a leader, what can you do when you realize this has happened?

Break out a list of plans, gather two other people to create a committee of three, and put them in priority order.

Once prioritized, triage them – decide which are best to abandon, and which are best to renew efforts toward. It's okay to have a middle pile of "maybes."

I recommend picking just one or two to renew efforts on. When you've picked them, include the important tasks as a part of your regular agenda, and get them done.

Also, formalize your decision to abandon the ones you're leaving behind; this shows the team that it's okay to change course, and it's better to be deliberate about it.

Going forward, what can you do to keep this kind of thing from happening?

From the beginning, make sure each task has an owner—a specific person to ensure it gets done—and a clear deadline.

During every meeting, spend a minute on each plan or task – just ask the owner for a one-color status update:

- **Green – it's on track to meet the deadline.**
- **Yellow – it's at risk of falling behind.**
- **Red – it is behind.**

If it's yellow or red, ask the owner "what help do you need from anyone here?"

Then, act on the answer. Come up with a way to help, so that it gets done; you've already decided it's worth doing.

If it's green, smile and say "thanks - keep up the great work!"

Rate yourself – and ask others to rate you – on this:

To move along planned initiatives, I work with my team to prioritize, toss out, assign ownership and deadlines, and regularly check in on them.

(low)   1   2   3   4   5   (high)

Self-perception:

_____

_____

_____

Feedback from others:

_____

_____

_____

_____

_____

9

DECIDE: STOP, START, CONTINUE

Another quick way to move forward is to do a simple "Start, Stop, Continue."

Do this: put up 3 pieces of chart paper, and label them at the top with "START," "STOP," and "CONTINUE".

Have on hand:

- calendar of events, activities, recurring projects
- a list of current projects or initiatives
- if you have them, lists of recurring tasks for each position

As you comb through those lists, you can put them on the "stop" or "continue" sheet — most will end up in the "continue" category.

Discuss any possible "stop" nominations. Most organizations have some dead weight somewhere.

For example, you could stop...

- a social media account that has no interaction or followers, but has become a time suck.
- a rule requiring people to make it to a certain number of events, because no one is enforcing it anyway.
- making locker signs for every single event, because everybody locker front has become a mess of posters, and the hallway looks sloppy, not spirited, because of it.

Then, as your discussions unfold, there will inevitably be times when someone says, "Well, you know what we *could* do…"

At that point, you have new ideas to put on the "start" sheet. That way, ideas for new initiatives or ways of doing things arise organically, and not as a result of freewheeling brainstorming.

For example, you could start…

- bringing teachers treats on the mornings when you don't have school, but they have "staff development," whatever that is.
- having meetings where everybody stands up, because it seems to generate more active discussion.

Doing a "Stop, Start, Continue" can provide renewed focus and great ideas.

Rate yourself – and ask others to rate you – on this:

Sometimes, I use a simple "Stop, Start, Continue" to keep myself, and the team, on track.

(low)   1   2   3   4   5   (high)

Self-perception:

_____

_____

_____

Feedback from others:

_____

_____

_____

_____

_____

10

● ● ●

WRITE EFFECTIVE GOALS AND HELP OTHERS TO DO SO

You don't have to look too far to find information on how to write goals. But sometimes the process can intimidate you, or push you in the wrong direction.

Another great way to write effective goals is to ensure that just two important elements are included:

1. Specific actions.
2. Timelines and/or deadlines.

For example, let's say I've been grumpy, and have been late to practice. I'd better change!

Three approaches – in order of effectiveness:

Avoid: "I'm going to be better at getting to practice, and more positive about our work."

Better: "This month, I'm going to get to practice on time, and start saying more positive things about my teammates."

Best: "I will be on time for practice every single day, and on Wednesdays, I'll make sure to come 5 minutes early. This trigger will remind me to find a positive comment to share with at least two people. I will do this each week for a month, then come up with a new goal to make a habit of."

It's much easier for others to hold you accountable to the third approach. And, the use of triggers can really help.

Rate yourself – and ask others to rate you – on this:

My goals are specific, and include timelines or deadlines to keep me accountable. *Bonus points for helping your teammates set goals this way, too. *

(low)   1   2   3   4   5   (high)

Self-perception:

_____

_____

_____

Feedback from others:

_____

_____

_____

_____

_____

SECTION THREE: INTEGRITY

Integrity

Does it go without saying that leaders must have integrity? Maybe it just can't be said enough.

The leaders at Iowa's Character Counts have a great way of looking at character in your personal life linking to character in your leadership life:

If having character in your personal life — moral character — can be called being your "best self," then having character in the workplace — performance character — can be though of as doing your "best work".

Consistency in decision-making and the way people are treated builds credibility and develops relationships. The constant practice of staying mature in the moment, and treating others with dignity, furthers those relationships.

"Leadership is serious meddling in other people's lives" – Max DePree

Rate yourself – and ask others to rate you – on this:

I have high moral standards, and my actions are consistent with those values.

(low)　　1　　2　　3　　4　　5　　(high)

Self-perception:

_____

_____

_____

Feedback from others:

_____

_____

_____

_____

_____

11

● ● ●

DO WHAT YOU SAY YOU WILL DO

In their research on Characteristics of Admired Leaders, Kouzes and Posner found this: Far and away, the most desired characteristics of leaders are (in this order):

Honest, Forward-Looking, Inspiring, and Competent.

It's fascinating that both "inspiring" AND "competent" are on the list together, as frequently a person in a leadership role demonstrates one characteristic but not the other.

What really stands out is that out of all the things a leader can be, HONEST is at the top of the list.

How do we prove that we are honest?

Here's how: Do what you say you will do, or DWYSYWD.

Do you expect people to be fully involved in meetings? Then keep YOUR phone put away during a meeting.

Do you expect people to show up for practice on time? Then, YOU must show up early (and leave last).

Do you expect fellow players to push their hardest, even at the end of practice? You guessed it — YOU must work even harder.

Early in my career as a band director, I had a little trouble with this. There was no food or drink allowed in the band room. And if students violated this rule, I gave them detentions. I got mad when students tried to sneak around this rule by having candy behind their stand. Fair enough, right? Well, I'm leaving out a part of the story.

Every day, I had a bottle of Diet Coke. I even had a little spot for it on a shelf under my music stand. You students can spot a hypocritical double-standard a mile away, can't you? You bet. I had no credibility when I came down on students for having that food. And I didn't get it.

I was an ineffective leader, and this double standard was one example of what was holding me back.

Do what you say you will do, and actively demonstrate your core values.

Rate yourself – and ask others to rate you – on this:

I follow through on what I promise to deliver; I Do What I Say I Will Do.

(low)   1   2   3   4   5   (high)

Self-perception:

_____

_____

_____

Feedback from others:

_____

_____

_____

_____

12

● ● ●

ACTIVELY DEMONSTRATE YOUR CORE VALUES

Have you flown on a plane? If you have, you know it's not the ideal experience that you may have pictured before your first flight. Unpredictable things happen, and you often have no choice as to who you are sitting next to, and space is tight. If you've got a big "space bubble," it can be tough.

Once, on a two-hour flight, the man sitting to my left accidentally jabbed me with his elbow – repeatedly.

I'm empathetic; he was in the middle seat. Still, there are "rules," and he was often in my space. With his elbow, with his newspaper, and with his leg and foot. He was a textbook example of the self-centered, inconsiderate plane passenger.

Eventually, he put the paper away, and pulled out a notebook. I confess, I peeked.

He was working on his personal values. No kidding – at the top of the page he was studying, and writing notes on, his guiding value:

"Love my neighbor as myself."

He wrote many lofty goals, like "volunteer at the homeless shelter downtown." His intentions were clear, and good, but his current product?

Inconsiderate foot, leg, and elbow contact. I wanted to chime in and say, "I've got a GREAT idea on how you could show courtesy to your neighbor." But that would be level two on the Maturity scale, at best, so I just huddled closer to the window.

Does your team, club, or organization have "core values?" Probably. But – do you *live* them? The best way to answer that question is to totally define what they look like in these areas:

1. Personal work
2. Team work
3. Output

For example, when I was a band director (during a more successful phase of my career than the one I told you about in the last reading), our group had this motto:

"The most important thing we do in band is treat each other with *kindness* and *respect.*"

How did that look, when we were at our best?

1. Even when criticizing, people talked to each other *kind*ly.
2. People didn't eat food in class (*respect*ing the classroom and their instrument).
3. When I stopped the music playing to address the class, people paid attention and listened quietly and *respect*fully.

Pick any value, and come up with examples in those three areas, then give (and seek) feedback on how well they are executed.

Push yourself and your organization to set values. If they already have them, then learn about them. Talk about them on a regular basis. It's worth it.

Rate yourself – and ask others to rate you – on this:

My words and actions demonstrate my organization's core values.

(low)   1   2   3   4   5   (high)

Self-perception:

_____

_____

_____

Feedback from others:

_____

_____

_____

_____

_____

13

AVOID STUPID RULES

When I was young, I had a teacher, Mr. Henry (not his real name), who had an obsession with headings.

Every assignment that was turned in was required to have a heading, and it had to follow the same exact format every time:

> Name
> Date
> Class
> Homeroom
> Assignment

And it had to be in the upper right hand corner. If it wasn't, it wasn't accepted. You'd get a ZERO. This was a small school. There were only four homerooms. If these four teachers didn't have their homerooms memorized by the third day of school, I'd be surprised. And I think the class would be obvious by the assignment. Math problems are difficult to mistake for Language Arts. But if you turned in your math assignment without putting "Math" on the third line of the heading, guess what? ZERO!

Oh, and did I mention that this was fifth grade?

Mr. Henry wanted to instill discipline. He wanted each piece of paper to have a clear intention. What he got was fear and rebellion. And he always seemed frustrated.

These well-intentioned policies (note that they did have a rationale) worked against the relationship he had with each student, and actually contributed to a lack of cooperation.

He even prided himself on the occasional "fun days" he had. But those weren't refreshing; they were confusing. Because it just didn't fit.

And that's the problem; when the rules fail to match what the group supposedly stands for, it results in confusion, or even a serious lack of integrity.

If you are leader, captain, president, or section leader, take a look at the rules or traditions that seem to not make sense. Eliminate stupid rules, perhaps those you don't follow yourself, and ensure that everything you do reflects your values.

Rate yourself – and ask others to rate you – on this:

I evaluate the rules my team follow, and work to adjust them if they are unfit to reflect our values.

(low)   1   2   3   4   5   (high)

Self-perception:

_____

_____

_____

Feedback from others:

_____

_____

_____

_____

_____

14

● ● ●

ASK: HOW DOES THAT MAKE YOU FEEL?

You've already heard me talk about Disney Parks. And you'll hear me talk about Disney again for sure. One cool thing that Disney does is share their secrets about how they do things, and do them well, at classes (expensive ones) held by the "Disney Institute."

At the Disney Institute, participants are challenged to think about how their decisions as leaders or team members make others *feel*. That seemed basic to me, even insulting, until they pushed us to take a closer look.

Most of us think about how big things make people feel — we're sensitive during that tough conversation, we make decent small talk when we can tell that it makes others more comfortable, etc.

But what about little things? Especially routine things?

On small things, do you turn your full attention to someone, or do you multitask?

When you send an email or text, is it a pleasant experience for the reader?

Do you force people to work with your way of doing things, or do you bend to match the ways of others?

As I listened to the Disney speaker, I still thought that paying attention to the feelings of others was a strength of mine; after all, I train people on this stuff!

As we all talked to each other, however, I was challenged on a few things:

Does your process leave people feeling glad to work with you, or do you make it a routine chore?

This was the big one:

What parts of your routine, your relationships, your teamwork, have you never, ever given any thought to, in terms of "How does this make them feel?"

This really challenged me.

I went down to Disney just a few weeks later, and noticed some things:

A staff person took a silly request for a spare charging cord extremely seriously.

A waiter sensed that something was wrong with my dish and replaced it before I could awkwardly complain.

I also recalled the time I was hot, and tired, and got snarky when I was asked if I needed anything at a drink cart at one of the Disney Parks. I said, "Yeah – you got any overpriced soft drinks?"

Without skipping a beat, that server made me feel awesome. She said "Sure! Want one for free, though?"

What? Really?

"Okay..." I was wary, but she had my attention.

"Order it in Whale."

"Whale?"

"Yeah, like Dory in *Finding Nemo*."

I did it. I smiled. I got a free Diet Coke, and since I played ball so nicely, they even offered me a free ice cream bar.

Here's the thing; all these examples require no special skills, just habits of thoughtfulness. And they can make a BIG difference in the commitment of those around you.

Have more influence by paying attention to how everything, big or small, makes people feel.

Rate yourself – and ask others to rate you – on this:

I am attentive to how people feel when interacting with me, even on small-scale, or mundane work.

(low)   1   2   3   4   5   (high)

Self-perception:

_____

_____

_____

Feedback from others:

_____

_____

_____

_____

_____

15

BEWARE THE SUCCESS DECEPTION

Some of the best teachers I know are people who struggled through school. Some of the weakest teachers I know, conversely, experienced a lot of success. Adversity strengthens us, and success can fool us.

In my first of three band director jobs, things didn't start out very well, but after about three years, I "figured it out," developed a system, and made things work for that group of 26.

Then, I moved to a new school, and tried the same system for a group of 118. Again, things didn't go very well at first, but after three years, I "figured it out," developed a new system, and things worked for that group.

Then, I moved to a new place, tried the same system...

You know where this leads, right? When a leader experiences success, two deceptions occur:

1) This system works! Therefore, it will work everywhere. I've got it all figured out!

2) My approach to people works! Everyone should act like I do, then they will also be successful!

Leaders deluded by this false sense of success are dangerous, because their [justifiable] self-confidence prevents them from entering a mode of self-improvement.

I was in this mode (the wrong one) under my second boss, who told me years later "Man, you couldn't tell that guy (young Alan) *anything!*"

Success deception causes two big problems:

1. Stagnating development, and
2. Lack of appreciation of different approaches from others, leading to judgment, or lack of trust.

Please note: This is not about how *young* you are. This is not "you'll understand better when you are older." Hear this: I spend a *lot* of time talking to my corporate clients about this topic. In fact, young leaders like you are sometimes less likely to fall victim to the success deception. But you are not immune…

Enjoy success, but beware of its deceptions. If there is a sweet spot when it comes to personal growth, it's this: "I know I don't know it all, but I'm open to learning more." The most successful leaders, young and old, embrace this.

Do you suffer from the Success Deception? Ask your coach/advisor/director, the teacher who knows you best, and your best friend. They'll let you know.

Rate yourself – and ask others to rate you – on this:

I remain open, conscious, and aware of my methods. I never rely on them for an assumed future success.

(low)   1   2   3   4   5   (high)

Self-perception:

_____

_____

_____

Feedback from others:

_____

_____

_____

_____

_____

SECTION FOUR: COMMUNICATION

If there's one skill that leaders must master and habitually improve above all, it's communication.

So many problems, drama, misunderstandings, and performance failures can be traced directly to communication missteps.

It's tough to summarize this one, but here's an attempt:

Communication goes out, and it comes in.

To keep both channels flowing freely:

Communicate *out* with practiced skill:

- Write well.
- Speak clearly and specifically [with solid presentation skills].
- Ensure that your body language is consistent with your message.

Communicate *in* with conscious deliberation:

- Read carefully.
- Listen actively [with verbal, physical, and visual affirmation].
- Be mindful of the tone, body language, and personality style of the speaker.

"The only way to lead when you don't have control is to lead through the power of your relationships." – Margaret Wheatley

Rate yourself – and ask others to rate you – on these:

I listen well, with total focus on the speaker.

(low)   1   2   3   4   5   (high)

I speak well, clearly, specifically, in a way that leaves no question what I meant and that shows total respect to the person listening.

(low)   1   2   3   4   5   (high)

When helping or correcting someone, I address a person's specific actions, not his or her attitude.

(low)   1   2·   3   4   5   (high)

Self-perception:

_____

_____

Feedback from others:

_____

_____

_____

_____

16

BE SPECIFIC BY USING THE BEHAVIOR-OUTCOME STATEMENT

In peer-to-peer student leadership, you must avoid being bossy. You know this. But then, you might be afraid to address problems. Here's the secret solution for you.

When addressing anything, be specific. Most importantly, make it be about the behavior, and the outcome. The outcome is important because it answers the question "Why?"

Brain research and common sense teach us that people are more willing to buy into something if they know the reasons why. Instead of a long explanation, this can be accomplished quickly and casually by mentioning the outcome.

Being specific is important because it reduces the likelihood of misinterpretation. We often know exactly what we need, but because the person we are talking to isn't psychic, we have to spell it out.

Talking about behavior, rather than general mood, or mindset, or attitude, keeps it real. Also, if it is something negative, this keeps it from being too personal.

So, when addressing things, *be specific*, state the behavior, and state the outcome. We call this the **behavior-outcome statement**. In each pair of examples, the second one is more specific and focuses on behavior and outcome.

[weak] Kate, your attitude sucks this week.

[strong] Kate, when you groan loudly after everything that coach says, it makes the freshmen think it's okay to disrespect coach.

[weak] Tim, you're so awesome!

[strong] Tim, when you smile and say "hey" to the newbs, they're glad they're here. That gets them to work hard right away.

[weak] Isaac, you don't really seem to care about getting here on time, and I'm getting sick of it.

[strong] Isaac, when you show up late for meetings, we don't get as much done because we don't want to start without all the officers.

[weak] Javier, great! You're finally showing some commitment get here on time. Thank God.

[strong] Javier, ever since you started coming earlier, it seems like coach is happier and we get started quicker. Sweet work, bro.

Speaking specifically, and in terms of behavior and outcome, takes a bit more mental energy, and even some planning ahead.

Making it a habit will make you more effective and increase your influence.

How can we still sound nice (good thing), casual (good thing), and offer a deadline (good thing), and get better results (very good thing)?

By being specific and making a request. Great phrase for that request: "Will you please...?" This still gives people a choice, theoretically, but you won't find a "no" very often.

A scenario:

"Hey, Isaac, we've got to do better about getting stuff done at meetings. It's second semester already. **Will you please** make sure to get here at 7 instead of 7:10?"

"Well, I'll try. I suck at mornings."

"Is there anything I can do to help make it happen?"

"Well, since you asked.... will you pick me up at 6:45?"

"Sure."

Can you picture that? Sure! It's all still casual, nice, with specificity, and a request. With a bonus "Is there anything you need from me?" thrown in for an extra measure of support.

Kindly, casually, make specific (very specific) requests. See what happens.

Rate yourself – and ask others to rate you – on this:

When addressing behavior (good or bad), and making requests, I communicate with specificity, and always state an outcome.

(low)   1   2   3   4   5   (high)

Self-perception:

_____

_____

_____

Feedback from others:

_____

_____

_____

_____

_____

17

• • •

CREATE CLARITY

Few things are more energizing than leaving a productive meeting with your club, set ablaze with fresh ideas that will set the wheels in motion. You're ready to go. Your team is ready to go. You've established goals and are ready to tackle the world.

It's a great feeling. Until something, somewhere gets a little hazy.

Clarity, a close cousin to specificity, is a valuable follow-through quality that can easily get lost in a drive of enthusiasm. Clarity ensures that everyone is on the same page. While specificity identifies important information (like who is doing what and when it's due), clarity ensures all of the questions are answered before anyone even gets started.

Clarity especially falls victim to sloppy meetings when everyone *thinks* they're in sync. Sometimes we think everyone understands the situation and tasks, and no one asks clarifying questions (either because they think they already know the answer, or worse, they think they're the only one who doesn't understand and don't ask out of fear).

So how can you avoid falling into a haze of doubt and worry? ***Follow up.***

After the meeting has concluded, make sure notes or minutes with action items go out within 24 hours if possible. Encourage members to respond with questions, additions or changes from their own recollections. It can only add to the picture. Use email, Google Docs, or whatever is easiest.

Make a habit of checking in with members individually before due dates. One-on-one conversations create a safer environment for asking questions. Keep it friendly and casual, like "Hey Hira, have you called that reporter yet about covering the awareness walk?"

Clarity is a fancy word, isn't it? You don't use or hear it much. But you're a leader, and you get to know these kinds of things. Clarity keeps the energy of momentum going. It anticipates questions that could come up later. Make clarity a priority and your results (and your team) will benefit.

Rate yourself – and ask others to rate you – on this:

I consistently follow-up on the tasks and initiatives my team is working on.

(low)   1   2   3   4   5   (high)

Self-perception:

_____

_____

_____

Feedback from others:

_____

_____

_____

_____

_____

18

REMEMBER: ATTITUDE IS NOT EVERYTHING

I love this quote from *Batman Begins*:

"Bruce, deep down you may still be that same great kid you used to be. But it's not who you are underneath... it's what you do that defines you."

I cringe when I hear someone try to pump people up with an "attitude is everything" approach.

While it sure is helpful to our own motivation to have a great attitude, it is unwise to focus on the *attitudes* of others, especially as a cure-all.

Why?

Sometimes, a person can have a great attitude, but be a negative influence on others. If I enter a group with an excited, take charge, can-do attitude, I might be totally ignoring the personalities of the other members. What if the other people like to take a slow, mellow approach?

And what if that's the best way? My attitude might just mess things up, or at least show disrespect.

This can harm relationships and get in the way of achieving things. Then, what I learn is this: having a great attitude is a bad idea. This isn't totally true; using inconsiderate *behavior* is a bad idea. A subtle and critical difference.

Some days, a person can have a terrible attitude. If that person has learned that "attitude is everything," then on that day, that person might not try. If a team member thinks, "My attitude is terrible today, so I am useless," then their contribution will surely suffer, *and* their day will probably be lousy. That person is wrong about attitude: if their *behavior* contributes, then that is what matters, and can move the team forward, even on a bad day.

If you are the leader, and you see a "bad attitude" on your team or in your section, it is generally useless to address the attitude, because it is vague and personal to them. However, if you focus on the *behavior*, you can experience success. Consider these two approaches:

[weak] "Hey Brett, shape up that attitude! You're bringing everybody down. Fire up!"

[strong] "Say Brett, when any of us acts grumpy by frowning and avoiding questions, that brings us down and the freshman really start slacking. Sorry you're having a rough day, dude. We need you, though, so can you push harder and really tell us what you think, please?"

Focus on *behavior* instead of attitude and see what happens.

Rate yourself – and ask others to rate you – on this:

I focus on the behavior of my team members. If efficiency or production is falling short, I address behaviors, rather than attitudes.

(low)   1   2   3   4   5   (high)

Self-perception:

_____

_____

_____

Feedback from others:

_____

_____

_____

_____

_____

19

● ● ●

ENCOURAGE INITIATIVE BY ASKING FOR IT

When I work with teachers, advisors, coaches, and their top student leaders, I frequently hear this frustration: "I want others to initiate more on their own — to do more of what needs to be done without being asked." Well, here are two truths:

1. You have to ask. Early in the year or season, very specifically. Later, it can be as simple as "You are expected to initiate things and not wait to be asked. What is one thing you know you could do — and would do if asked — but aren't doing right now?" People aren't psychic. So, ask for what you want.
2. Do you want to be elected, or appointed as a leader, or get other awards in the form of scholarships, titles, opportunities, or unique letters of recommendation?

Initiate things without being asked. Self-starters WIN, because they are rare. You are the person that everybody wants to hire, promote, honor, and/ or be around.

Be psychic, and do what your leader needs without being asked.

This is an attempt at a challenge, and is meant to be helpful:

Leaders who complain about their followers being "lazy" because they don't initiate more might be perceived as "lazy" by observers, because they aren't doing the hard work of asking and guiding.

Rate yourself – and ask others to rate you – on this:

I actively guide my team in the right direction of what work needs to be done (without assuming they should just know). OR If I ever think "they should <u>know</u> that," I spell out what I'm thinking.

(low)   1   2   3   4   5   (high)

Self-perception:

_____

_____

_____

Feedback from others:

_____

_____

_____

_____

_____

20

AVOID SAYING "SHOULD"

There is a class of words we ought to avoid, as they can crush individuality and show a lack of trust. These may include "ought," or "must," but let's focus on the one that seems to pass the most judgment:

"Should."

"Ought" is a little softer, and "must" is so strong that its intention is more obvious.

"Should," however, is more ominous, and implies something about the speaker's attitude toward the listener's ability to make their own decisions.

Can you feel it — the judgment? The moral superiority?

"You should go to Wartburg College's camp."

"You should get a Snapchat."

"You should start writing your papers sooner."

"You should run for secretary, not president."

You're thinking – But what if it's the truth? Doesn't it make sense to talk that way? No.

"Should" implies superior knowledge. "Should" implies superior judgment. And "should" can deny personhood.

Instead, say:

> "A camp I thought about was Wartburg's – want to hear more?"

> "If you have Snapchat I can send you videos from the concert."

> "If you start earlier on your paper, you'll have more time for the final edit." (Note: this is a behavior-outcome statement.)

> "You're the best writer in the club. We could totally use your mad skills as secretary."

Using the behavior-outcome model:

If you avoid using the word "should," you'll give people more dignity.

or

When you say "should," here's what happens; you rob the other person of dignity.

You get the idea.

Rate yourself – and ask others to rate you – on this:

I am careful to eliminate the word "should" from any directions and suggestions.

(low)   1   2   3   4   5   (high)

Self-perception:

_____

_____

_____

Feedback from others:

_____

_____

_____

_____

_____

21

AVOID SAYING "DON'T"

Don't say don't.

Really. Two reasons for this:

1) Some research shows that the use of words/phrases involving "not" or "-n't" are subconsciously turned into the positive by the listener, because negative talk is rejected. So if a person is told "don't be late!" they actually perceive "be late," increasing the likelihood of non-cooperation.

2) Consistent negative talk will create a negative culture. A constant drumbeat of "don't forget" "don't be late" "don't screw that up" "don't talk to me right now" can be pretty discouraging. If you can rephrase things using positive words, a better atmosphere is created. Better atmosphere = more encouraging = more productive.

Lots of words can be used to address behavior you want to stop.

Stop, avoid, limit, resist the temptation to, watch out for, etc.

Throw in a courtesy word, and you've gone from ogre to friend, without lowering your standards:

"Please stop texting during the meeting."

"Limit your talking to the topic, please."

"Always arrive on time, please."

"Please remember to turn in the form by noon."

And of course…

Please avoid use of the word "don't."

Rate yourself – and ask others to rate you – on this:

I am careful to avoid using the word "don't" when directing my team members.

(low)   1   2   3   4   5   (high)

Self-perception:

_____

_____

_____

Feedback from others:

_____

_____

_____

_____

_____

22

● ● ●

AVOID SHUTTING DOWN COMMUNICATION

Leaders avoid saying things that shut down discussion and communication.

The temptation is strong. Sometimes, when you're ready to move on, you may use one of the phrases below to be efficient. Or, you're not at your best and you're anxious to get out of the conversation.

Whatever your reason, the impact of these words will send the message that you want to shut the exchange down. Using them can be damaging to your credibility.

Here are some examples:

"...Enough said." Or the slang version "'nuf said."

"Last time I checked," followed by something like "this was still a free country."

"Just sayin'"

"No offense, but..."

"Yeah, BUT..."

A great alternative to the last one is "yes, *and...*" or, "maybe... it's *also* true that..."

In your next give-and-take, especially if it's heated, ask yourself (or put on a sticky note in front of you):

"Are my words shutting down the conversation, or keeping it open?" And remember to sometimes just say, "I don't know – what do YOU think?"

Rate yourself – and ask others to rate you – on this:

I make a conscious effort to keep discussion and communication open, rather than using phrases that might shut it down.

(low)   1   2   3   4   5   (high)

Self-perception:

_____

_____

_____

Feedback from others:

_____

_____

_____

_____

_____

23

* * *

AVOID SAYING "INAPPROPRIATE"

We started this section with Reading 16, which addresses the value of being specific.

One word that seems like a good one to use, but is more vague than you think, is "inappropriate."

Usually, "inappropriate" is being used as a substitute for something more specific and something better. Take that opportunity to make a more suitable (i.e. specific) substitution.

Leaders use "inappropriate" because it's safe; it doesn't force them into getting specific, and it might spare offending someone or making someone feel micromanaged.

Stop taking the easy way out, and use something more specific instead. Here are a few detailed examples to help you practice –

Avoid saying: "Those comments were so inappropriate. I don't want to hear anything like that again. Is that clear?"

Instead, say: "Telling Shawna that her idea 'sucks' isn't the way we talk around here. Next time, please find better words, and definitely avoid 'sucks' in the future. Okay?"

Avoid saying: "Please don't hold fundraising meetings in inappropriate places."

Instead, say: "Next to the dumpster behind the school is a bad place for a committee meeting. Have it in a place where it's easier to take notes. If you're unclear, please ask. Thanks."

Avoid saying: "Stop with the inappropriate emails to the percussion section."

Instead, say: "Emails filled with emojis, exclamation marks, and inside jokes among the upperclassmen make the freshmen feel left out and wonder what the heck is going on. Please stick to the facts in the mass emails, and save the fun for personal stuff."

Using the word "inappropriate" as a catch-all is too vague. Define what you really mean in order to connect with others, get to what's needed, and increase understanding.

Rate yourself – and ask others to rate you – on this:

I avoid using the word "inappropriate" to describe someone's behavior because there is a better, more specific description for their actions.

(low)   1   2   3   4   5   (high)

Self-perception:

_____

_____

_____

Feedback from others:

_____

_____

_____

_____

_____

24

NEVER BE SARCASTIC. EVER.

When I was in 6th grade, my music teacher, Mr. Jones, played music from something called *Switched-On Bach* – 17th century composer J. S. Bach performed on synthesizer.

That was pretty cool back in 1980. It was like the first hints of EDM. It actually got me really interested in actual Bach music – I'm a fan to this day.

Mr. Jones was a real advocate, and fed me more to listen to, and encouraged my unusual (for a 6th-grade boy) passion for Baroque music. Until one day...

The big payoff at the end of the year (if we were good) was the "Rock and Roll Filmstrip Series." (You probably don't know what a filmstrip is. Google it and laugh at my generation's ancient ways.)

When Mr. Jones announced this was coming, he said offhand, "Then there's Alan. All he wants to listen to is Bach!"

Classmates laughed, of course. Mr. Jones smiled at me, as if to say "Just kidding. I know you can handle it. I only 'pick on the people I really like.'"

I was embarrassed, sure, but more so, I felt betrayed. Who was this guy? Was he the one who encouraged my Bach passion, or the one who made fun of it? Jerk.

Fast forward to recent history, where I am the jerk:

After one witty exchange with an acquaintance, in which I was extremely funny (really, quite hilarious, I assure you), my wife said to me:

"You know, when you're sarcastic, it keeps people guessing. Even people who know you well. Do you really want that?"

No. Who am I? The one who encourages genuine connection and positive relationships (for a living!), or the one who uses them for cheap laughs? Jerk.

Effective leadership requires positive relationships, which require genuine connection, which isn't possible with sarcasm, or "only picking on the people you like."

"But I'm young! I'm in school!" you say, "That's how we talk!"

Me too. But only with my closest friends, and *never* when it's time to lead or work in a team.

There is no place for sarcasm in effective leadership. Humor, yes! Sarcasm – picking on people – no. Sorry. While it may be hilarious, it keeps people guessing, and wary.

And you don't want that.

Rate yourself – and ask others to rate you – on this:

In an effort to encourage genuine connection with my team, I avoid using sarcasm.

(low)   1   2   3   4   5   (high)

Self-perception:

_____

_____

_____

Feedback from others:

_____

_____

_____

_____

25

KNOW WHEN TO AVOID GIVING FEEDBACK

Feedback from leaders drives involvement and performance, but many student leaders still avoid it, because it can be an uncomfortable skill; you're worried about being too mean, or doing it wrong. Hopefully, the readings in this section have helped you with ways to do better in this area. But sometimes, you're right to hold back.

Here are two reasons why it might be wise to delay giving feedback:

"I've been piling on – everything I tell this person has been critical lately; I feel badly about that."

This is an important realization – look in the mirror. If you've been focusing on the negative and avoiding the positive, then make an effort to find ways this person has contributed, and acknowledge them with positive feedback. Once you achieve balance again, give the corrective feedback.

Another possibility, though, is this; there is truly nothing to give positive feedback about. In that case, it's time to ditch the casual feedback and get formal. This may be a time for you, as a student leader, to step back, inform your adult sponsor or coach, and let them do the job.

Is there a middle ground between those two options? Probably not. This is either a big, tough moment for you, or for them. Something needs to change. If you don't have the relationship power to do it, turn it over to the formal authority. Here's another reason to hold back:

"I'm in a bad mood, and I'm going to come across grumpy."

Good move. Give no critical feedback if you will end up seeming even slightly more mad than you actually are. The receiver of feedback exaggerates that emotion on their end, and will end up feeling far more corrected than you intend.

There are two ways to deal with this:

1. Wait until you are in a better state of mind.
2. Give a lot of appreciative or positive feedback to people around you. It will improve your mood. Research shows that a 3 to 1 ratio of positive to critical feedback is effective for keeping people involved. This will be re-emphasized in upcoming readings.

Rate yourself – and ask others to rate you – on this:

I am careful not to give corrective feedback when I am in a "bad mood".

(low)   1   2   3   4   5   (high)

Self-perception:

_____

_____

_____

Feedback from others:

_____

_____

_____

_____

_____

26

LEARN MORE ABOUT BEING SPECIFIC FROM DISNEY'S CUSTOMER SERVICE MAGIC

Something that strikes most visitors to Walt Disney World is how nice of a place it is. It's very clean. The employees are called "cast members" because they're playing a role and they have a reputation for great service and friendliness. Everyone knows that. And, you've already heard me talk about Disney in Reading Four.

But there's something else to point out. The guests at Disney World seem to be better behaved, happier, and more positive than customers at other places of business and entertainment. Most of us probably think this is because of the cleanliness and friendliness of Disney and its staff. But there is something else at play.

In Reading Sixteen, "Be Specific," we talked about the "behavior-outcome statement". The staff at Disney—the cast members—use behavior-outcome statements also. All the time.

A couple of examples:

"Please move all the way down, filling in all available space–front to back and left to right–to make room for everyone."

At a lot of places where people need to make room like this, announcements usually sound like this: "Squeeze in, people." Most people would probably sort of comply. But, the Disney version offers the outcome (to make room for everyone) and that gives people a reason why. Further, the command itself begins with the pleasantry, "please," and is also very specific. Specific behavior + polite words + reasonable outcome = willing cooperation.

Some attractions start with a pre-show. This creates the great illusion that your experience is started– even when it hasn't. In one case (Ellen's Energy Adventure), there's a short film shown in a large carpeted open space. On a hot day, before the film started, I sat down on the floor. Mara (my daughter) laid on the floor beside me with her head on my knee and Julie (my wife) laid down on the floor in the other direction with her head on my other knee. It was a lovely family moment, but it was soon shattered by the cast member's announcement:

"If you are lying or sitting on the floor, please stand up. We need to make room for anyone else who comes in, and anyone who comes in will be entering a dark room from the bright outside, so you know, they might step on you. So, please stand for the whole eight-minute pre-show."

In other places, a staff member would likely make an announcement like "Stand up everybody. No sitting or lying down in here." But the Disney way involved the specific behaviors, and the specific reason why, along with a bonus; we were told exactly how long we would be standing. Despite the pleasant comfort of our position, we cheerfully obeyed.

Next time you go to Disney World, watch for this. It is a great example of organization members, exhibiting leadership behaviors, even though they aren't officially leaders.

If people at the lowest level of an organization (front-line employees) can motivate people outside of the organization (guests) with proactive communication that focuses on behavior, imagine how effective it can be if such an approach becomes the norm in your team or organization, and for you as a leader.

It can be magic.

Rate yourself – and ask others to rate you – on this:

I consistently make requests using specific language to describe behavior in the behavior-outcome model.

(low)   1   2   3   4   5   (high)

Self-perception:

_____

_____

_____

Feedback from others:

_____

_____

_____

_____

_____

27

KNOW HOW TO GIVE CRITICISM

Criticism is received fairly well when the relationship is strong. Coach John Robinson said, "Never criticize until the person is convinced of your unconditional confidence in their abilities." In other words, Coach was never critical of a person unless he had faith in them, and they knew it.

When I think of the people in my life that I willingly take criticism and feedback from, without taking it personally (though my family and friends may point out that I still get a bit defensive), I realize the following:

They have faith in me.

Think of the people who get defensive when you address or criticize them. Do they KNOW without a doubt that you have TOTAL faith in them? Or are they normal, and somewhat (or a lot) insecure?

Once you get to a great peer-to-peer respectful relationship, and they know you believe in them, you can start to give critical feedback. Until you hit that point, it will be less effective; in fact, you may lack the "relationship power" that we talked about in reading 4.

IMPORTANT: Continue to give positive feedback to reinforce that faith, at a ratio of 3 to 1, positive to critical. Make it specific, and allow it to stand on its own. Look out for "Hey, great job with [praise], *but* next time you better [criticism]. "

Combining criticism with positive feedback in this way will backfire; your peer will see this mixed message as your lack of faith that they can handle the criticism, or that your positive feedback is a manipulative attempt to soften them up for the real criticism.

Rate yourself – and ask others to rate you – on this:

I consistently give positive feedback in a ratio of three to one, positive to corrective.

(low)   1   2   3   4   5   (high)

Self-perception:

_____

_____

_____

Feedback from others:

_____

_____

_____

_____

_____

28

IGNORE THE TONE

"**S**upreet, please remember to get that cart ready for the granola bar give-away the morning of the big standardized test."

Supreet [delivered with sarcastic tone and an eye roll]: "Well, sure, why not, that's the *greatest* thing Student Council does. Last time, the stupid freshmen took way more than their share, and when I was yelling at them, somebody grabbed the cart and rolled it behind the vending machine when I wasn't looking. [This is where the eye roll comes in] I can't wait to be in charge of *this* again."

Because sarcasm has no place in teamwork, you might be tempted to address the sarcasm. Or, the eye roll. Or, the clear resistance to a simple task that's part of a Student Council tradition. While that would be understandable, let's think "level 4"…

You have an opportunity here to send a message about ignoring sarcasm and having no time for silly pushback.

Do this instead. Totally ignore the tone of voice and focus on the message, being careful to avoid passive/aggressive tone yourself, and reply:

"Great. Thanks for taking care of that. I know you think it's a waste; next meeting, let's spend a few minutes on some ideas to avoid that the next time around. Thanks for your time."

In that response, you've:

1. Ignored the tone, yet showed that you heard the concerns.
2. Kept things positive, even though Supreet wanted to inject drama.
3. Taken advantage of an opportunity to be an ally and a problem solver (needs-meeter).

It's good to address tone of voice and enforce high standards of respectful communication, and it makes sense to do so at another time, so Supreet doesn't feel beaten up.

Stay alert for these opportunities.

Rate yourself – and ask others to rate you – on this:

When met with sarcasm or other blatant pushback, I ignore tone and focus on the message while acknowledging frustrations.

(low)   1   2   3   4   5   (high)

Self-perception:

_____

_____

_____

Feedback from others:

_____

_____

_____

_____

_____

29

GET TO KNOW PEOPLE ONE-ON-ONE

So much of this book is about building and using the influence that can only come from building relationships. There are no shortcuts to this, and it cannot be done in group settings alone.

You have to talk to people. You have to get to know them. You have to listen to them. And they have to get to know you, too.

So, make it happen regularly, make it happen deliberately, and make it happen comfortably.

Of course, you will "click" with some people more than others, and some people will resist your attempts. Be careful, and resist pushing too hard with shy peers.

Here are some safe topics that will help you get to know someone without being too invasive:

Home and family (Is Sheyenne your sister? Where do you live?)

School (How do you like Ms. Washington? What science are you in?)

Work (Do you have a job anywhere? Do you get good discounts?)

Other activities (Are you in a spring sport also? Did I hear that you do drama, too? Are you more xBox or PS?)

Music listening choices (do you like folk rock? Popular? Musicals? What's your jam?)

Usually, you start going off on enough tangents that you don't need to be too prepared with these topics and questions, but if you are nervous about the approach, these can help.

Rate yourself – and ask others to rate you – on this:

I talk with my team members one-on-one on a regular basis, and know a lot about them.

(low)   1   2   3   4   5   (high)

Self-perception:

_____

_____

_____

Feedback from others:

_____

_____

_____

_____

_____

30

SAY IT ALL

A marching band story:

Tykeshia was Tyler's section leader. She said things to him like "hold your saxophone out," "stand up tall," and "use your ring finger for the alternate f-sharp fingering in the chromatic passage."

All true, all helpful, but all critical. One day, Tyler said "Why do you hate me so much?"

Tykeshia replied, "I don't. I think you're great. I just know you can handle me being picky. You're doing just fine."

Tyler looked back to Tykeshia and summoned his courage, and said, "I'm sorry. That just doesn't work for me. I need to know when I'm doing things right, too."

Something that leaders often think is, "I don't need to tell people when they're doing things right. That's just their job. It's almost insulting to give compliments about the normal stuff they do."

There may be some truth to that, but this is also true:

People need to know how they're doing. It engages and motivates them.

This is also very true: research shows that people thrive more when they receive three bits of positive feedback for every one bit of corrective feedback. (But not all at the same time. That would be weird.)

If both of these things are true, then this makes sense:

Give people positive feedback when they're on the right track – even if it's just affirmation that they are doing things correctly. They'll stay more engaged, because they'll know they're on track, and be more receptive to critical feedback when it occurs.

Both of these improve engagement, and improve relationships. Once Tykeshia started telling Tyler both the correct things he was doing, the things he needed to improve upon, both Tyler's morale and their relationship improved. Tykeshia enjoyed working with Tyler more, because open communication builds strong relationships, and keeps people from guessing and stressing.

So go ahead and tell people when they're doing things right. Bonus: it also shows you don't take them for granted.

Rate yourself – and ask others to rate you – on this:

I regularly affirm my team members when they're doing what's expected.

(low)   1   2   3   4   5   (high)

Self-perception:

_____

_____

_____

Feedback from others:

_____

_____

_____

_____

_____

SECTION FIVE: MODELING

Leaders must consistently model the behavior they expect from others.

Modeling flows directly from integrity. Integrity is the leader's *commitment* to consistency. Modeling is the *display* of that commitment through behavior. Let's revisit examples from reading 11, with that in mind:

If you expect fellow players to push their hardest to the end of practice, then you must work even harder.

If you expect people to show up for practice on time, then you must show up early (and leave last).

If you expect your meeting participants to keep their technology set aside during meetings, then you'd best never get yours out, either.

"People look at you and me to see what they are supposed to be. And, if we don't disappoint them, maybe, just maybe, they won't disappoint us."
– Walt Disney

31

• • •

MODEL THE BEHAVIOR YOU EXPECT

Once, I planned a youth event that took place at a hotel, and I needed to check in eight rooms at once. The front desk was busy, and so I understood that I needed to wait my turn. No problem. However, the two employees checking people in were *not* moving very quickly. It was as though they felt no sense of urgency at all, and with a full lobby. It's not that they were thorough, they were... *slow*. And kind of cold. This made me a touch impatient. Then, the manager (well-dressed, cheerful, smiling) arrived on the scene, and I was momentarily relieved.

Momentarily.

Because here's what I pictured:

The manager would swoop in, station himself at the middle, unused computer, smile and say "Who's next?" And, because I was next, I would step up, tell him about the eight rooms I needed to check in, and he would smile, and say something like "I can take care of that for you," and proceed to very *obviously*, and very quickly, and very efficiently **show those other two employees how it's done around here.** With a smile!

Here's what *actually* happened:

Manager: "Have you been helped?"

Me: "No, not yet, but that's okay – it's busy, huh? Lots of birthday parties, it looks like."

Manager: "Yeah, it's crazy."

Me: "I just need to check in eight rooms."

Manager: "EIGHT!?"

Me: "Yup, I've got a couple groups here."

Manager: [gesturing to the employee to his right] "Then *she* can help you." [laughs, turns away, and leaves.]

Seriously.

So, I waited longer. No problem. They were busy. Plus, they were doing things exactly as they had learned around here. What more could I expect?

The next morning, the breakfast room was locked. I went to the front desk to let them know that it was locked. Simple oversight, and simple to fix, right? It just needed to be unlocked by 8:00 a.m.

It was unlocked at 8:20, with 40 hungry teenagers waiting patiently for breakfast.

It was a nice place, with nice people. What would it be like if the managers modeled the behavior that ought to be expected?

Have you ever seen the cars of a train pass the engine? Never.

If you're a leader, and you do things at level 10, your followers will likely do them at an 8. If you have a rough day, and your effort is a 7, expect your followers to be at a 5.

Leaders model the way by setting the example for others in ways that are consistent with their values. This promotes consistent progress and building of commitment.

Let's get to work!

Rate yourself – and ask others to rate you – on this:

I consistently lead by example, actively demonstrating the behaviors I request from my team.

(low)   1   2   3   4   5   (high)

Self-perception:

_____

_____

_____

Feedback from others:

_____

_____

_____

_____

_____

32

KNOW YOU'RE BEING CONSTANTLY OBSERVED

I once ordered a coffee from someone who made no eye contact with me, and waited for me to initiate the order with no greeting.

I had watched this go down with the three people ahead of me in line, also. They stepped up, placed their orders with the cashier, who looked down with her finger poised above the buttons. As the order was placed, she kept looking down, and spoke only these words: "Is that it?" and "Three fifty-six" (or whatever the total was).

The other thing I witnessed was this: she had a small problem and had a question for her supervisor. She looked at the feet of the supervisor, sideways, when she asked for help.

The supervisor gave a curt, nearly rude answer, while looking the other way doing nothing in particular.

Aha!

On the way out, I saw a "now hiring" sign that said "looking for workers to make a day-brightening experience for our customers!!!"

At some point, this woman had surely been told to provide better, more proactive service, but she didn't see that from her leader.

People don't do what we ask them to do.

People do what they see their leaders do.

Rate yourself – and ask others to rate you – on this:

I remain aware that my team <u>and</u> customers may be observing me even during routine moments, and I stay consistent even then.

(low)   1   2   3   4   5   (high)

Self-perception:

_____

_____

_____

Feedback from others:

_____

_____

_____

_____

_____

33

DO THINGS FOR THOSE YOU LEAD

Remember that two-word definition of leadership – "Meet Needs"?

You can really put that into action by staying conscious of things that you can do for the people you lead.

They are so used to you being the one to tell people what to do, that it's a nice change of pace when you ask them specifically,

"What can *I* do for *YOU*?"

Perhaps you've asked for a fundraising report from the treasurer. You could say, "Would you like me to help you go through those papers?"

Maybe you've put someone in charge of calling a DJ for a dance. You could say, "I have some time to help – do you want me to look up some online reviews?"

Consider asking your team occasionally, "What can I do to help YOU?"

Rate yourself – and ask others to rate you – on this:

I seek to meet needs by occasionally asking people what they need from me to help with their tasks.

(low)   1   2   3   4   5   (high)

Self-perception:

_____

_____

_____

Feedback from others:

_____

_____

_____

_____

_____

34

● ● ●

SHARE, ABUNDANTLY

When you lead, you're probably good at what you do. Most cross country captains run fast. Most trumpet section leaders play well. Most FBLA officers do well in class.

When you're good at what you do, others may ask for help. And, at first, you might say "yes" to those requests a lot. But look out for this: After a while, you might start to want to say "no." Fight that.

One reason you might start saying "no" is this: You're running out of time to help everyone who comes to you for assistance. Once one freshman trumpet player realizes that working with you helps her playing, pretty soon a half dozen others start asking for your time, and eventually you feel like a little teacher with all your spare time before school going away.

Find a way to keep saying "yes." Maybe you work with more than one person at a time, maybe you work with them less frequently, or maybe you make your help sessions shorter. But leaders meet needs, and these people need you. Be flattered that they ask for and want your help.

The more sinister and icky reason you might say want to say "no": Competition.

The insecure part of you might resist helping others get better because they might start to threaten to outshine you. And then, you might worry that your leadership role will be less valuable or that this other person might become more influential.

Two thoughts on that: First, it probably won't happen. You'll work hard enough to stay ahead, if that matters. But even if you don't, you'll still be that needs-meeting person, and that counts for a lot.

And second, even if it does happen - they start to do better than you - help them anyway. It's the right thing to do. It's not about you - it's about the organization.

Rate yourself – and ask others to rate you – on this:

When asked for help by my peers, I openly and abundantly share whatever I can.

(low)   1   2   3   4   5   (high)

Self-perception:

_____

_____

_____

Feedback from others:

_____

_____

_____

_____

_____

35

MASTER NEW SKILLS

**To know,
and not do,
is to not yet know. - Karl Lewin**

Have you ever explained how to tie your shoes? Better yet, was there ever a time that you tried tying shoes simply based on a verbal description of the process? You had to DO it to get it, right? That's what this quote from Lewin is getting at.

Have you ever heard a new leadership idea, or practice technique, or play fake that you couldn't wait to implement? Sure hope so! Ever given up because it was clumsy - or because the process intimidated you? You're not alone.

It is true that we ought to try new things. It is also true that when we do, we might be lousy at them. Lots of people give up at that point. The successful don't. They push through the clumsy attempts at new good ideas — and end up setting themselves apart from the crowd, just because they stuck to the new way of practicing spiking, or running a meeting, or executing the play fake.

Flip it around — do the people you lead nail everything the first time? Probably not. Do you make it safe to make mistakes, AND maintain the high standards that they must reach after they push through the mistakes? That's the sloppy, clumsy part of nailing new skills.

It's sloppy, though, to not coach others – and ourselves– after a mistake, failure, or clumsy attempt.

Here are some debrief questions:

- How can this lesson apply to others who will try this?
- What will you do differently next time?
- What could someone else on the team do to help you next time?

Feel free to explore other questions, but make sure they're focused on the future and the next opportunity.

It's useless to know, unless you do. Push through, and make it safe and expected for others to DO as well.

Rate yourself – and ask others to rate you – on this:

I make it safe for myself and my team members to make mistakes along the way.

(low)   1   2   3   4   5   (high)

Self-perception:

_____

_____

_____

Feedback from others:

_____

_____

_____

_____

_____

SECTION SIX: STRETCHING AND GROWING

—Stretching and Growing—

Leaders are committed to constant self-improvement.

Why use the phrase "stretching and growing?" Growing isn't descriptive enough. Anything that grows has to change; nothing just "gets bigger." There are changes, and some of them can be uncomfortable, even painful.

In order to grow, we have to "stretch." "Stretching" implies action, reaching, pushing, and willingly entering into discomfort and attempts to change. So, leaders have to stretch in order to grow.

One of two things is *always* true:

1. I am a perfect master of all my desired skills and capabilities; I'm perfect. Or,
2. I still have room to grow.

If you fall in category number 2, then what are you going to do about it? What are you going to do differently tomorrow than today?

What specific personal growth efforts do you consistently undertake? Who do you stay accountable to?

The best leaders have ready answers to those questions.
"You can't think yourself into a new way of acting; you must act yourself into a new way of thinking." — Clifford Madsen

Rate yourself – and ask others to rate you – on this:

I acknowledge that I always have room to grow, and consistently work to add new skills and abilities to my repertoire.

(low)   1   2   3   4   5   (high)

Self-perception:

_____

_____

_____

Feedback from others:

_____

_____

_____

_____

36

● ● ●

STAND OUT

In preparation for a breakout session at a conference for college students, I developed a list of things a leader can do to stand out and get noticed. Not in a "look at me!" kind of way, but in a way that will help the leader connect more to others, and to enable others to connect as well.

Some of this guidance appeared in earlier readings, but they are presented here, together, as we start to explore active stretching and growing, with a specific eye toward your future.

1) Never have the last word.

Strong leaders are tempted to consider many discussions to be arguments or debates – opportunities to change hearts and minds. A leader named Dale Carnegie said it like this – you can never win an argument. If you lose, you lose. If you win, you lost. Letting others have the last word will empower them and *set you apart* as thoughtful.

2) Avoid using earbuds/headphones in public.

Not because it's rude, or associated with a younger generation, or because it may appear to be a selfish attempt to control your own environment; but because it interferes with your ability to connect. *Set yourself apart* by always being open to connection.

3) Use skillful writing mechanics.

The proliferation of fast electronic communication has made it acceptable to abbreviate words and truncate sentences. FWIW -> I do it 2. Sometimes. This is good news – it makes it easy to *set yourself apart* by using traditional methods like complete words and sentences. I heard an anecdote once about a college professor getting an email from a student who had to get out of a commitment. It was two paragraphs, well written. Think that student set herself apart? Absolutely. He couldn't stop talking about how impressed he was by this student. And note, the student was writing to get out of a responsibility, and ended up not looking like a slacker because she wrote well!

4) Habitually use pleasantries and good etiquette.

Another casualty of speed and shortened communication is the use of "please", "thank you", and "you're welcome". Great news! If you make those words, and other polite words, your habit, it's easy to *set yourself apart*. "You're welcome" is the huge one; it conveys so much more openness and connecting than things like "yup" or "no prob," and honors the "thanker" more than "no, thank YOU."

5) Whenever possible, communicate by phone or in person.

Consider the number of chats and texts you deal with on a daily basis. Yes, they're convenient, but it's hard for any of them to stand out.

What if you are the person who makes conversation the default? You'll *stand out*. Warning — you might be annoying, too, if the person you're working to connect with much prefers the written word. Use with good judgment.

6) Stand in such a way as to be trusted and accepted.

Without going all-out on body language, just consider these two ideas: stand with your arms at your side (not in pockets, not crossed in front or back, not fidgety). Might feel weird at first, but research confirms this posture conveys the most openness and trustworthiness. Also, face the person speaking. Fully. Imagine a line from your nose to theirs – and keep it perpendicular to your shoulders. *Set yourself apart* by being the best-connecting listener. (Exception - in confrontational or negative feedback situations, consider standing side by side - it's easier to take.)

7) Never interrupt.

Ever. Most people interrupt, and it's normal. *Set yourself apart* by never doing it. Makes people feel valued.

8) Take every opportunity to write hand-written notes.

Especially to say thank you. It's a lost art, and doesn't take much time. However, it conveys that you've taken time and care, and this impression will help you *stand out.*

9) Never be sarcastic.

It makes people wonder how you really feel. This uncertainty interferes with connection. *Stand out* by being sincere.

There are lots of ways to set yourself apart, to be sure. But these nine have the most payoff, based on how easily you can implement them.

If you set yourself apart, you will connect better, and with more people. Then, you stand a greater chance of doing some good in the world.

And remember, these tools are always to be used for good and not for evil. In every interaction, you have the power to make the world a better place. Why not do it?

Rate yourself – and ask others to rate you – on this:

I can cite examples in three of these areas where I set myself apart.

(low)   1   2   3   4   5   (high)

Self-perception:

_____

_____

_____

Feedback from others:

_____

_____

_____

_____

_____

37

● ● ●

SOLVE INTERNAL FEUDS

When I was a young teacher, I often found myself in the middle of student disputes. My response was always something along the lines of "You need to learn how to solve your own problems." I was thinking I was doing them a service by empowering them to grow up and solve problems on their own. In reality, I was avoiding drama myself, and being selfish. Leaders of organizations need to clean up spats between people.

It is a cop-out to say "People need to solve their own personality issues," or "That's just the way he is; nothing I can do to change him."

These responses undermine the power of leadership. Also, you've missed an opportunity to improve the way your team works together.

If you have people in your organization who are too immature to solve their drama, then you have an opportunity to develop your people by teaching them how.

You also have a chance to demonstrate that you care, and that you're interested in seeing their lives become better. This is practical advice that will improve the effectiveness of your team, ensuring that more work gets done.

Effective leaders will understand that there are different personality styles. They also teach people to communicate and work in ways that connect with others, regardless of style.

Because that's what it usually is – a misfire of communication that leads to misunderstandings, that people inevitably chalk up to "personality conflicts," or immaturity.

Regardless of what you call it, the effective leader will step in to solve internal feuds.

Rate yourself – and ask others to rate you – on this:

Instead of using the old "solve it between yourselves" strategy, I take the opportunity to lead by addressing drama between people.

(low)　　1　　2　　3　　4　　5　　(high)

Self-perception:

_____

_____

_____

Feedback from others:

_____

_____

_____

_____

_____

38

● ● ●

MAKE CLUMSY ATTEMPTS TO DO THE RIGHT THING

Clumsy attempts at self-improvement are better than smooth successes at staying the same. One good example of this for you is the process of giving positive feedback.

Most young leaders understand they should try new ways of giving feedback, but they don't do it.

The most frequent obstacle, it seems? Discomfort.

You know from previous chapters that great leaders provide frequent, specific, behavior-based feedback that is more often positive than negative.

So if I know it helps to say things like, "Maya, you always do a great job getting the plyometric platforms ready for volleyball practice. Thanks, keep it up," then why don't I?

Because it's not a habit.

If I know it is actually non-threatening and relationship-building to say things casually like "Hey, Maya, it really helps the freshman know to start conditioning right away when the platforms are up – will you please make sure to get here early to do it?" then why don't I?

Because it's not a habit.

Make it a habit, right? Easier said than done.

Because the first time, it might come out like

"Maya – um, hey – Maya. Yeah, I was meaning to say, ah, that those newbies are working hard right away when they get to practice. And part of that is cuz you get the plyo platforms up each day. And it's super helpful, even though it seems like a little thing. So um, keep doin' it, okay?"

And it feels clumsy, and may make you uncomfortable.

Too bad. Leaders need to push their comfort zones to do uncomfortable things.

And Maya appreciates it. Because what would you normally say? Nothing. And Maya doesn't know how she's doing. Because you never tell her. Because it's not a habit yet.

An amazing thing is this:

At one point in time, Michael Jordan was a lousy ball player. At first, Miles Davis had lousy trumpet-playing skills.

At one point, you couldn't read. Clumsy attempts are needed before good things – then great things – happen. Make them. That's what leaders do.

Rate yourself – and ask others to rate you – on this:

Although it may feel clumsy and awkward, I make a consistent effort to make giving positive, specific feedback a habit.

(low)   1   2   3   4   5   (high)

Self-perception:

_____

_____

_____

Feedback from others:

_____

_____

_____

_____

_____

39

● ● ●

BE TRANSPARENT (WITHOUT TMI)

Transparency builds trust. Too many leaders have a habit of holding back information, which can look like information-hoarding, or secret-keeping. Those behaviors hurt trust.

But, leaders also know when to stop; leaders will avoid the temptation to share TOO much information. Leaders share information, as appropriate, to:

A) keep people informed,

B) keep people from wondering, and

C) show your confidence and security.

Example of information-hoarding:

"Everything is fine and will continue as always around here. Don't let the rumors get to you."

Example of transparency:

"I've also heard the rumors that Student Council is going to get disbanded for some reason. Mr. Goldstein said the administration is talking about it and we will know for sure next week."

Example of over-sharing:

"Yeah, my mom knows someone on the school board who told her that the administration is cutting all school clubs that don't serve enough of a purpose, and all they think Student Council does is put on dances and raise money for little things that no one cares about. And Mr. Goldstein might retire next year so they could cut us and no one would really care. So maybe we should be scared. I'll keep you posted because I hear all the rumors and I'll pass them on."

Where's the line? It's easier to find when you've had more experience. Until then, consider this:

You might share too much information when

- you are insecure

- trying too hard

- overly stressed

- looking for sympathy.

Rate yourself – and ask others to rate you – on this:

I make certain not to under or over-share information, particularly when stressed or insecure.

(low)   1   2   3   4   5   (high)

Self-perception:

_____

_____

_____

Feedback from others:

_____

_____

_____

_____

_____

40

● ● ●

KNOW THAT ALL SOLUTIONS ARE TEMPORARY

Jill was a jerk of a choir section leader.

The altos didn't like her, mostly because she was bossy, passive-aggressive, and a bad communicator.

This all added up to a low-trust, high-tension situation.

Jill got good advice from a leadership workshop: Be nice. Build relationships. Build trust. Avoid bossiness.

It worked. For a while. Until the altos started to fall behind. People took advantage of "nice Jill" after they realized she really had changed. Jill was frustrated again, for a new reason.

"Am I too nice, now?" She asked for more advice. And she got good advice: Ask for more. Without being bossy, be in charge; set goals, maintain high standards in the sectional practices you lead, communicate clearly and ask for more.

And it got better. Way better. Jill finally realized that all solutions are a temporary resting place.

We never really have it all figured out. Sometimes, things go well, and we get lulled into complacency, thinking that now we've stumbled across "the formula."

But people evolve, situations change, and the circumstances of the changing world dictate that we stay nimble, self-aware, and ready to adopt a new point of view.

Sometimes it's enough to just build relationships. Sometimes it's time to be encouraging. And then, it makes sense to ask for more.

Rate yourself – and ask others to rate you – on this:

I remain self-aware, ready to adapt when new solutions need to be formed.

(low)   1   2   3   4   5   (high)

Self-perception:

_____

_____

_____

Feedback from others:

_____

_____

_____

_____

_____

SECTION SEVEN: POSITIVITY

Positive Passion!

We've covered six leadership traits and skills. Now, it's time to talk about two mindsets that must permeate our leadership behaviors.

The first is positivity. Being positive is the way others see that the hard work is worth it.

Now, a leader ought not be fake and weirdly smiley; positive leadership is not soft leadership. It *does* mean that leaders generally use positive language, display optimism, and treat people kindly.

It is also not enough to simply preach a "positive attitude." While it *is* possible to control our attitude, and a positive attitude *does* make our day better and work easier, those around us do *not* see our attitude; they see our behavior.

So – have that positive attitude. Good plan. If it's a bad attitude day, though, you are not defeated. Stay positive in your words and body language around others, so they understand that the hard work is worth it.

"When enthusiasm is inspired by reason, is practical in application, reflects confidence, and spreads good cheer, raises morale, inspires associates, arouses loyalty, and laughs at adversity, it is beyond price." – Coleman Cox

Rate yourself – and ask others to rate you – on this:

If you ask the people I interact with, they will tell you that I am optimistic.

(low)   1   2   3   4   5   (high)

Self-perception:

_____

_____

_____

Feedback from others:

_____

_____

_____

_____

_____

41

● ● ●

KNOW POSITIVE LEADERSHIP ISN'T "SOFT" LEADERSHIP

Sometimes people are skeptical about a positive approach to leadership. Some seem to equate "positivity" with being super-nice, but being kind is much deeper than giving empty compliments like "good job" or "nice work" or "super!"

You can't be too kind. But, you *can* be too soft. That is the difference. In the book *Good to Great,* Jim Collins uses the phrase "rigorous, not ruthless." This is the message for leaders who would like to be positive.

Remember the "behavior-outcome statement" model from reading 16? This focus on behavior, and the high standards of your organization, can be done in a way that is positive, not negative. In a way that is rigorous, not ruthless.

There is a danger in being nice while enforcing high standards. If one continually says things like "please be quiet" or "I am just assuming that all this nasty behavior has a purpose" with a smile, you will seem passive-aggressive, which is on the edge of sarcasm, and sarcasm has no place in leadership; it is cheap and disrespectful. However, you don't have to be angry or stern either. Team members who "buy in" will be more productive *and* more loyal.

One other way to enforce high standards and be kind is to remain very specific about behaviors. Saying to the whole wrestling team "we all need to make sure we stay until the mats are cleaned", when there's just one or two people sneaking out early, does not help the cause. That is soft *and* negative at the same time.

Taking aside the wrestler who skips out early and saying, "You nearly always do what you're supposed; you're gonna be taken more seriously when you stay till the end. Around here, we stick around, unless there's something else going on that I don't know about. Is there anything wrong I need to know about?" This sort of correction validates the employee's contribution and enforces the high standards. If your tone of voice is matter of fact, then you will *not* be stern, or mean.

Because everyone has experienced so much stern or grumpy correction from some teachers and coaches, a matter-of-fact correction or criticism will, over time, become part of a positive approach. An approach that upholds high standards *and* is very specific about behavior is positive, *but not soft*. Be rigorous, not ruthless.

Rate yourself – and ask others to rate you – on this:

I uphold high standards and maintain a positive environment by being specific about desired/undesired behavior.

(low)   1   2   3   4   5   (high)

Self-perception:

_____

_____

_____

Feedback from others:

_____

_____

_____

_____

_____

42

BEWARE ACTING WHILE STRESSED

Everything you do makes a person's day better or worse. What are you going to do with that power?

Once, I got a car wash. The car was fairly new and the paint was intact at that time — no dings or scratches yet. When I examined it a bit later, though, I found a scratch. A very small hairline scratch, perhaps two inches long, just above the rear driver's side door. Barely noticeable, but real, and clearly caused by dirt or sand being in the brushes of the car wash. I required justice.

I was having a busy and stressful day, and this really put me over the edge. I complained. I was given a form to fill out to request compensation. It didn't get results, so I returned, days later, and met with the owner. The owner and employee were slow to respond, and I got a little passive-aggressive in the interactions, and a couple weeks later, they finally relented to my pressure and complaints, and set up an appointment for me at a body shop for paint retouching for the scratch. Justice!

I'll bet I spent four hours on the issue, and put an extra 20 or so miles on my car, but I got Justice! And I felt terrible. It had taken a long time, I had to be a bit of a jerk, and it really wasn't that big of a deal. My stress (and, frankly, feelings of powerlessness) had gotten the best of me.

Recently, while getting gas, I bought the add-on car wash at the pump. Just $8. When I pulled around to the car wash, though, it was being cleaned and was out of operation for the next couple hours. When I went to the cashier inside to get my money back, I was told that the car wash was a separate business, and that I'd have to call the owner. I did, and left a message about the situation. He didn't call me back for four days, and apologized for how long it took him to get back to me. I said this:

"No problem. Hey, if I was obsessing over this thing, I'd probably have some pretty messed-up priorities." He was really thankful for that attitude, and said that he wished everyone were so easy to deal with. He made the situation right.

Justice! But this time, I felt better. Because I had treated the "offenders" better.

I wouldn't mind bumping into the last guy sometimes. But the previous car-wash people? I'd hide my face and hope they didn't remember me.

80% of decisions are made based on emotion, not reason. Also, we tend to act less mature when stressed. The lessons? There are many.

One is this; when stressed, see if you can delay acting, or speaking, or addressing a situation until the stress passes. This will increase the likelihood of a better decision, and (more importantly) better interactions and relationships. Be nice.

Rate yourself – and ask others to rate you – on this:

I respect the interactions I have with people by holding off acting when stressed until a time when I can communicate with even temperament.

(low)   1   2   3   4   5   (high)

Self-perception:

_____

_____

_____

Feedback from others:

_____

_____

_____

_____

_____

43

● ● ●

USE THE PHRASE "AROUND HERE..."

The first principal of my teaching career was fond of saying, "Most days, we have fun **around here**." The first time I heard him say this was in my job interview. He followed it up with, "...and you can't say that about most jobs."

It was my first job, so I took his word for it. He was right, but I think part of the reason he was right was the consistency and relentlessness of his message, and the subtle pep talks he gave. By using the words "around here," he was painting a picture of the school's atmosphere/culture/vibe all the time, and it was also a way of controlling the school's atmosphere/culture/vibe.

Smart. And like all smart ideas, worthy of using in other situations. You can use it too.

Back when I was a teacher, I started saying variations of, "The most important thing we do **around here** is treat each other with kindness and respect." I said it a lot, put it on written communication from time to time, and eventually it stuck. The students repeated it on cue.

It caught on, I think, for two reasons:

1. It was basically true most of the time, for most people.
2. It was a worthy goal that spoke to the needs of the people in the group.

It wasn't just a slogan, or a cute bit of indoctrination. It had a positive impact on our culture, and became the way we enforced our standards. This can work for you, too.

For example, if Tina lets her rough day get the best of her and she snaps at Laura, you could say, "Hey, Tina – I'm bummed that you're having a bad day, but that's not how we treat each other **around here**, no matter what. Is there anything I can do to help you?"

When you add that last part, mean it sincerely. If Tina says, "I need time away from everybody," give it to her.

Even things as simple as punctuality or accountability can be put into the culture.

"Say, Dylan, **around here**, we show up on time. Any reason you're late that I need to know about? Are you okay?" Asking those last two questions indicates that you have faith in Dylan, assuming the best of him, and that you regard his behavior as the exception, not the rule.

Assume the best about people, and you will generally receive it.

Rate yourself – and ask others to rate you – on this:

I actively participate in creating/maintaining our group culture by using the phrase "around here, we..."

(low)　　1　　2　　3　　4　　5　　(high)

Self-perception:

_____

_____

_____

Feedback from others:

_____

_____

_____

_____

_____

44

KEEP PEOPLE ON THE RIGHT TRACK

So far in the book, we've found several ways to communicate specific feedback, both positive and critical. Now, let's be even more clear about the purpose; and if you've become a believer, consider communicating all of this to your peers.

At some gathering, declare your intention to be more purposeful with feedback, both positive and critical. You might use words like these:

> "I have learned some things about peer leadership and feedback. I'm going to work to be specific with you all, to be unafraid to be critical, and to do a better job of letting you know you're on the right track by giving you lots of positive feedback. I'm aiming for a balance of three bits of positive feedback for each bit of criticism, and I'm not going to deliver all of it at once, but let each bit stand on its own."

If people are mostly doing what they're supposed to be doing, but only hear criticism, they will have the mistaken belief that they are doing a poor job. In an environment like this, morale, performance, and relationships suffer.

If people need criticism (or to be "asked for more") sometimes, but only hear positive feedback, they will have the mistaken belief that they're performing perfectly. That is until something causes a serious problem and takes them by surprise.

This will also hurt morale, performance, and relationships.

Most people do well most of the time. And, most people prefer to work in a positive atmosphere.

The simplest way to keep people on the right track is to remember…

Three to *One*: give three bits of specific, affirming feedback for each bit of critical feedback.

Too much negative will hurt, but so will holding negative back.

This ratio will keep the atmosphere positive, and give team members a realistic view on how they're doing.

It will strengthen their understanding of what to keep doing, and what to change.

Three to one. Give it a shot, be specific, and stay accountable to your peers.

Rate yourself – and ask others to rate you – on this:

I have told my peers of my intention to use a 3:1 ratio of positive to corrective feedback to maintain a positive, but effective, environment.

(low)   1   2   3   4   5   (high)

Self-perception:

_____

_____

_____

Feedback from others:

_____

_____

_____

_____

_____

45

● ● ●

REMEMBER THE WORK

Have you seen productivity dip while creating a positive atmosphere? There's a likely reason, and a solution.

So much of this book's content is devoted to positive, encouraging, servant leadership. Every once in awhile, a leader comes along who is so committed to positivity that they wonder why productivity might be down, not up. They're usually missing something...

The **work**.

The work *has* to get done. The whole point of positive, encouraging servant leadership (in the context of WORK) is more about creating an environment of engagement to *set the stage* and *right the relationships* to ensure that work gets done.

If you do encounter a slowdown, and blame it on a greater commitment to positivity, double-check yourself on these questions covered in the last reading:

Is at least 25% of your friendly, specific feedback *corrective*, rather than *complimentary*?

When someone consistently falls short of expectations, do you have a *habit of addressing* it, rather than ignoring it?

Make sure you're staying positive, but also communicating specifically and immediately when something needs to be done differently (or at all!).

Make sure no one ends up being complacent or lazy because you're afraid to deal with consistent issues.

Stay positive. Stay encouraging. Build real relationships. Meet needs. Then make sure the work gets done by asking for more.

Rate yourself – and ask others to rate you – on this:

In the midst of building positive relationships, sticking to new habits, and seeking to meet needs, I do not let the <u>work</u> get neglected.

(low)   1   2   3   4   5   (high)

Self-perception:

_____

_____

_____

Feedback from others:

_____

_____

_____

_____

_____

SECTION EIGHT: PASSION

Positive Passion!

Leaders must have passion; that is, in their own way, they must show that they care.

Talk can only go so far – while a pep talk can work sometimes, it's what you *do* that demonstrates your passion. There's a lot you can do to show your passion and commitment. Some ideas:

Approach everything you do with energy and determination.

Give praise for the efforts of peers.

Enforce high standards by providing timely, specific, behavior/outcome-based feedback.

Deliberately build your team – by working hard together.

Willingly do the "dirty work" and menial tasks that no one wants to do, but are absolutely necessary.

"Leadership is the art of mobilizing others to want to struggle for shared aspirations."

– Jim Kouzes and Barry Posner

Rate yourself – and ask others to rate you – on this:

If you ask the people I interact with, they will all tell you that I am passionate about our work.

(low)   1   2   3   4   5   (high)

Self-perception:

_____

_____

_____

Feedback from others:

_____

_____

_____

_____

_____

46

CHANGE THE PACE

I had a teacher who told us to "do everything 10% faster."

This guy had lots of energy, and got lots done. And, the students who followed this advice seemed to work harder, have more energy, and be happier. Over the last 30 years this advice has proven invaluable; it works for me, too.

Not only does following this advice generate more productivity, more energy, and more happiness, it also provides a needed change of pace. When we change up our pace and alter our routine, we become more aware of our work and become more productive.

Sometimes life gets frantic. Dr. Lee's advice dates from the middle of last century, and technology has caused us to accelerate our pace and our frequency of communication. So, while this idea of moving faster still makes sense, another bit of advice might be helpful when we stress:

Sometimes, do everything 10% more slowly. Changing the pace downward—downshifting— can help us reflect more, de-stress, become less frantic, breathe more deeply, and have more fun.

Effective student leaders will change up their pace, because they know it helps their energy and productivity. In fact, if you can't decide which direction you ought to change the pace, just pick one randomly. Just the change will help you reflect on whether or not it was a good idea.

Changing up your pace will help you get more done, have more energy, and enjoy life more. Give it a shot.

Rate yourself – and ask others to rate you – on this:

I periodically call for a change of pace - from myself or from others - to amp up energy and productivity, or reflect and de-stress.

(low) 1 2 3 4 5 (high)

Self-perception:

_____

_____

_____

Feedback from others:

_____

_____

_____

_____

47

●　●　●

SEND HANDWRITTEN NOTES TO PEOPLE

When I was a teacher, I didn't get a lot of handwritten notes from my students.

So when I did, it was pretty exciting…

I once got a note that was slipped without warning or fanfare. There was no significant event that precipitated it; she just wrote, "Thank you for making your office a safe place."

To think that any student would make the time to write words of appreciation or encouragement when a pop-by visit or high five might have been enough, really made a major impression and boosted my morale.

And, I bet that the act of writing the note made *her* feel better as well.

I once sent a handwritten note to a former colleague, thanking him for his informal mentorship and giving a couple of examples of how it was affecting my current practice. He responded by calling me, and we reconnected.

We both felt great, and motivated, and the act of writing and sending the note consumed fewer than five minutes.

Put a reminder on your phone every, say, three weeks to pick a teacher — or even a peer — to write a note to.

It will boost you, and them, and remind them that you notice and appreciate their work.

Rate yourself – and ask others to rate you – on this:

I send handwritten notes of thanks and praise to others.

(low)   1   2   3   4   5   (high)

Self-perception:

_____

_____

_____

Feedback from others:

_____

_____

_____

_____

48

● ● ●

ALIGN WORK WITH VALUES

In reading 7, we talked about rubrics in general as a tool to develop vision. Let's take that further to talk about a way to make your passion more obvious to others.

Examine all your responsibilities to your team, club, or performing group. These can include big projects, or routine tasks. Compare each of them to the goals and values of that team. Consider eliminating the ones that are not aligned with those goals or values. This is a way to focus your work in front of others.

Then, make sure the things you're doing are the ones you talk about, encourage others to do, and turn you into a role model.

For example, if your band has a goal to learn the music for the whole marching band show by September 10, then don't spend time on making encouraging lockers signs on September 8; instead, go find every single player in your section who doesn't know their music yet, and do whatever it takes to get them to meet the September 10 goal.

Then, turn that process into a story of success at your next leadership meeting.

Make your efforts match your goals and values, then share success stories to show your passion for the work.

Rate yourself – and ask others to rate you – on this:

I check regularly to make sure my work is aligned with my organization's goals and values.

(low)   1   2   3   4   5   (high)

Self-perception:

_____

_____

_____

Feedback from others:

_____

_____

_____

_____

49

SPREAD PASSION WITH STORYTELLING

Tell good stories of struggle and success.

- They help you spread your passion.
- They help you keep the members of your team fired up.
- They keep you all focused on your purpose.

I was director of a band once that had a better-than-average year in marching competitions, and so they were very anxious to prove themselves at the last contest of the year, in Ankeny, Iowa.

It was cloudy, and it looked like rain was coming. We got organized and ready to enter the field anyway. While the previous band was performing, light rain began. As that previous band exited the field, our drum majors called the band to attention, ready to enter and compete for the last time. Then, the downpour began. The color guard flags became saturated and limp. The wool uniforms got heavy with rain. But adversity can motivate, and for some magical reason, the students stood straighter, and even more ready to enter the field.

10 minutes and a full inch of downpour later, the contest director came over to tell us how much he admired us, but that the contest was now cancelled. Frustrated, we got out of our soaking clothes and got on the bus for a very wet 2 hour trip home.

Seems like a bad ending, right? You'd think so, but after that, any time there was even a touch of complaining about adversity, some student (not me, which was cool) would say something like, "Remember Ankeny?" and students would stop griping and work harder. As the years went on, students made sure that incoming freshmen knew the story of Ankeny.

So, are you telling stories? Or, have you avoided them, because it's uncomfortable, or because it's too braggy and that goes against your desire to be humble?

Tell them anyway.

This is one way to stay passionate, and remind everyone why their efforts make a difference.

Rate yourself – and ask others to rate you – on this:

I tell stories to keep everyone fired up and ever mindful of our purpose.

(low)   1   2   3   4   5   (high)

Self-perception:

_____

_____

_____

Feedback from others:

_____

_____

_____

_____

_____

50

HOLD UP ROLE MODELS

Peer role models can be powerful tools for keeping that spark of passion alive in your workplace.

Notice the individual efforts that created some of your greatest successes – the things that motivate you and your peers to keep coming back.

As the student leader, and as someone who has read the "Modeling" section of this book, you may assume that the "role model" job is yours. You're right. But leaders have humility and make sure that the spotlight is on others.

So, note the role models. Praise them and hold them up. But be careful. Don't do this with know-it-alls or other people who are resented because of their arrogance - your efforts will have the opposite effect.

Instead, note the positive and humble over-achievers and make them your role models. Their success is more relatable and can help others see what you're shooting for.

Rate yourself – and ask others to rate you – on this:

I hold up role models to help motivate and spread passion for our work.

(low)   1   2   3   4   5   (high)

Self-perception:

_____

_____

_____

Feedback from others:

_____

_____

_____

_____

_____

NUMBER 51

Remember my mistaken assumption from the beginning?

"The last thing the world needs is another book on leadership."

I was wrong to resist the call to action and the push to provide this book. I hope it's been helpful, of course. But I still say

"There are plenty of books on leadership."

So what's not in this book? What's something you've learned somewhere else, that you know is essential for your leadership journey?

Record it here:

_____

_____

Create your own summary of this behavior at the top of the next page.

Rate yourself – and ask others to rate you – on this:

_____

_____

_____

(low)   1   2   3   4   5   (high)

Self-perception:

_____

_____

_____

Feedback from others:

_____

_____

_____

_____

Now go meet needs. Start now.
Thanks for reading,

Alan Feirer

REFERENCES

Arbinger Institute (2000). *Leadership and self-deception: Getting out of the box.* San Francisco, CA: Berrett-Koehler.

Block, P. (1993). *Stewardship: Choosing service over self-interest.* San Francisco, CA: Berrett-Koehler.

Carnegie, D. (1964). *How to win friends and influence people.* New York, NY: Simon and Schuster.

Collins, J. C. (2001). *Good to Great: Why some companies make the leap--and others don't.* New York, NY: Harper Business.

Disney Institute., & Kinni, T. (2011). *Be our guest: Perfecting the art of customer service.* White Plains, NY: Disney Publishing.

Greenleaf, R. K. (1991). *The servant as leader.* Indianapolis, IN: Robert K. Greenleaf Center.

Heifetz, R. A., & Linsky, M. (2002). *Leadership on the line: Staying alive through the dangers of leading.* Boston, MA: Harvard Business School Press.

Horstman, M., & Auzenne, M. *Become a Better Manager and Have a More Successful Career.* Retrieved from http://www.managertools.com/

Kouzes, J. M., & Posner, B. Z. (1993). *Credibility: How leaders gain and lose it, why people demand it.* San Francisco, CA: Jossey-Bass.

Kouzes, J. M., & Posner, B. Z. (1995). *The leadership challenge: How to keep getting extraordinary things done in organizations.* San Francisco, CA: Jossey-Bass.

Lautzenheiser, T. (1992). *The art of successful teaching: A blend of content & context.* Chicago, IL: GIA Publications.

Pink, Daniel H. (2009). *Drive: The surprising truth about what motivates us.* New York, NY: Riverhead Books.

Ury, William (2007). *The power of a positive no: Save the deal save the relationship and still say no.* New York, NY: Bantam Books.

Walter, Jr. Wangerin (1984). *Ragman: and other cries of faith.* New York, NY: Harper & Row.

Welch, Jack, Welch, Suzy. (2005) *Winning.* New York, NY: Harper Business.

ACKNOWLEDGEMENTS...

First, because this book is adapted from my previous work for corporate audiences, *The Group Dynamic Field Guide,* I need to again thank some people who made that work a success.

My wife, editor, and business partner, Julie Feirer, did most of the initial editing, and final editing, and some detail work. Ashleigh Rader, our assistant, did most of the detail work on the formatting and rearranging, and did a lot of editing, and catching little things, and putting up with me changing my mind about stuff a lot. Jordan Kuhns designed the cover, and has adapted it nicely for this version. Matt Pries has proofread and provided feedback for much of my writing and oral delivery over the last several years, and that work has left an imprint here. Melissa Miller ghostwrote some blogs for me a while back, and some of that content appears here.

Second, none of those people did any proofing of this version. Only teenagers—one in junior high, one in high school, and one in college—reviewed this version.

I'm so thankful to them: Mara Feirer, who provided four pages of picky notes; Jessey Wyzgowski, who very generously dug in even though we had never met face-to-face; and Zachary Walker, whose advocacy and engagement is an asset and blessing to everyone he touches.

Finally, Dr. Tim Lautzenheiser has assimilated so much work on motivation and leadership, and when I asked him once how he felt about me "stealing" some of his "stuff," he responded with "Is it being used to *build people?* If so, then *steal away!*" Done, sir. The Four Levels of Maturity have taken on a life of their own.

I'm also quite grateful to Tim for writing the foreword to this book, and for making student leadership his life's work. If he hadn't, I don't think I'd be on the path I'm on today. Anyone whose life has been impacted by Tim knows *exactly* what I'm talking about.

ABOUT GROUP DYNAMIC...

Group Dynamic sessions are designed to help leaders and teams get more done with less stress and interference. Learn more at **www.groupdynamic. net**. While my work as a teacher, and as Group Dynamic, has helped thousands learn about the concepts in this book, it is also true that I have learned much from all of my clients and students, and they have shaped me and the content. All solutions are a temporary resting place.

AFTERWORD

THE VIEW FROM ROCK BOTTOM

This is how Group Dynamic and my career in leadership training and development began.

It wasn't pretty, and hundreds of young people witnessed it.

The year was 1996, and I was despondent and irritated while I was at school, pretty much all of the time. I was in a well-earned and long-sought after band directing position, the biggest (perhaps the best) band program in our conference, but my students weren't engaged. They didn't get me. They weren't loyal. They weren't receptive, they weren't performing up to par, and they were quitting. It wasn't **my** fault, of course… They just needed more time to get to know me! Right?

Except… there were signs to the contrary.

My principal said, on several occasions, "They are fighting you," but instead of considering his comment thoughtfully, I dismissed him.

My colleague at the Junior High raged, in a moment when I'd pushed her a little too far, "They are tired of you acting like you're their *king!*" Geez, I thought. She must be jealous! I still didn't get it. I called my predecessor, Jim, to ask, "What's their problem? Why isn't this working?"

Jim knew the answer but was too diplomatic to hold up a mirror.

So, as any recent graduate with a master's degree might do, I turned to the books. Surely, research would tell me the answer. Thank goodness, the first thing I checked out of the library was *The Leadership Challenge* by Kouzes and Posner, and it quickly helped me diagnose what "their" problem was.

The problem was me. (I bet you saw that coming.)

SEEKING WISDOM FROM THE GIANTS

For a while after this revelation I was even more discouraged. But then, I started reading and digesting every relevant thing I could get my hands on. After *The Leadership Challenge* I read some other weighty stuff by authors named Senge and Greenleaf, some popular titles by Pitino and McGinnis, Covey and Carnegie. I took notes, outlined, highlighted, and made charts to track the commonalities between these authors and their ideas. I did all of this while supervising a study hall, pausing only to sign passes for seventh-graders.

It was rigorous in some ways, and most certainly nerdy, but it was also time well spent. Those notes, charts, and scribbles evolved into an 8-point leadership model that saved "my people" from me.

Passionate, motivated, and cheered by the success of that model, I began to share it with other band directors and their students. The response was overwhelmingly positive, and after about twelve years, that work became my full-time vocation in classrooms and board rooms around the Midwest and beyond. At first, I worked only with youth, but then expanded to grown-ups, too.

This book is a supplement to that curriculum, an introduction to the 8-Point Leadership Model that provides the foundation of my work with others in leadership, training, and organizational development.

ART AND THE ORIGIN OF THE 8-POINT LEADERSHIP MODEL

Prior to writing this book, I searched for the handwritten matrix I used as my crude research guide during that period of heavy reading and weighing ideas, so I could share a picture of it here. I'm bummed that I can't find it! I remember it all coming down to a "Top 4" and a "Top 8" — that is, four tenets that were basically undisputed, and four more with wide support that also resonated with me.

The top four were: ***Service***, ***Vision***, ***Integrity***, and ***Communication***.

The other four were ***Modeling***, ***Stretching & Growing*** (often called other things, like "Sharpening the Saw," or "Constant Self-Improvement"), ***Positivity***, and ***Passion***.

There were others that weren't universally identified as primary leadership traits, but rather behaviors, that seemed worthy of inclusion, such as "sharing the credit," "risk-taking," and "celebrating and encouraging."

At this point the content was shaping up but the format was unwieldy, and I realized I needed to get it organized. I needed help.

I called Art.

It's good to have someone in your life who can talk sense into you, to keep you humble while giving you support, to balance motivation with caution, and to stand above you on the balcony to give you the big picture.

For much of my college career, that was Art. He was caution to my impulse, calm to my hyper, and always let me make mix tapes from his eclectic CD collection. He was also our campaign manager when his girlfriend, Amy, and I ran for Student Body President/Vice-President. (We lost the election, but the two of them are now married with three awesome kids.)

Art was one of the absolute best "people" people I've ever known — and still is, by the way. His path led him to higher education, working in student life. He's a Dean of Students now, at Loras College in Dubuque, Iowa.

He was, and is, a great leader. So, when I was getting all impulsive and motivated to cram this curriculum together into a content-laden, un-digestible "leadership feast," I knew that Art could help me streamline it into something that made sense. He said something like this:

"Scale it down to six elements, and make it a triangle. Three on the points, three on the sides. Six. Easy to picture, easy to remember, easy to use.

"But I have ELEVEN!" I argued.

"Scale it down to six."

"Can't do it."

"Yes you can."

"Fine. Eight! Service, Vision, Integrity, Communication, Modeling, Stretching & Growing, Positivity, and Passion."

"Nope, too many. You could make it seven, and put one in the middle..."

"I'll combine positivity and passion, and stick 'Positive Passion' in the middle."

"Fine. That's seven."

"Eight."

"Fine."

Art is a great friend, and an amazing man. And since 1998, thousands of people have experienced this curriculum, and filled in their triangles in their handout booklets. But they don't know Art's role. That's okay with him; he is the picture of humility and lives to serve, not get kudos. But isn't that the way it always is with folks like Art?

So – credit where credit is due. I don't know where Group Dynamic and this leadership curriculum would be if it weren't for Art Sunleaf.

This book outlined the Group Dynamic Leadership Model that was born of my own pursuit of a more successful and rewarding relationship with the people I worked with, and emerged through research, development, and my work with Art. I hope it did well at taking you through each point in the model, fleshing out the importance of each and ideas for their real-life application.

If so, thank Art, Kouzes, Posner, Lautzenheiser, Senge, McGinnis, Horstman, and all those other giants whose shoulders we stand on.